Navigating the Fintech Frontier Transformative Innovations and Risk Factors in Financial Services

Edited by

Abdul-Razak Abubakari
Entrepreneurship and Enterprise Development
Tamale Technical University, Tamale, Ghana

Mohammed Majeed
Marketing Department
Tamale Technical University, Tamale, Ghana

Nurideen Alhassan
Accountancy Department
Tamale Technical University, Tamale, Ghana

&

Jonas Yomboi
Accountancy Department
Valley View University
Oyibi-Ghana

Navigating the Fintech Frontier Transformative Innovations and Risk Factors in Financial Services

Editors: Abdul-Razak Abubakari, Mohammed Majeed, Nurideen Alhassan & Jonas Yomboi

ISBN (Online): 978-981-5324-90-7

ISBN (Print): 978-981-5324-91-4

ISBN (Paperback): 978-981-5324-92-1

need for a court order if at any point you breach any terms of this License Agreement. In no event will any delay or failure by Bentham Science Publishers in enforcing your compliance with this License Agreement constitute a waiver of any of its rights.

3. You acknowledge that you have read this License Agreement, and agree to be bound by its terms and conditions. To the extent that any other terms and conditions presented on any website of Bentham Science Publishers conflict with, or are inconsistent with, the terms and conditions set out in this License Agreement, you acknowledge that the terms and conditions set out in this License Agreement shall prevail.

Bentham Science Publishers Pte. Ltd.
80 Robinson Road #02-00
Singapore 068898
Singapore
Email: subscriptions@benthamscience.net

BENTHAM SCIENCE

CONTENTS

PREFACE

In an era where technological advancements are rapidly reshaping industries, the financial sector stands at the forefront of this transformation. This book looked into the multifaceted world of financial technology (Fintech) and its profound impact on the banking and financial services industry. From the opportunities and constraints of Fintech adoption to the intricate dynamics of artificial intelligence, blockchain, big data, machine learning, and the Internet of Things, this comprehensive exploration aims to provide readers with a nuanced understanding of the ongoing digital revolution. By examining both theoretical perspectives and practical implications, the book highlights how these cutting-edge technologies are not only transforming traditional banking but also introducing new challenges and risk factors that must be carefully managed.

This book is intended for a diverse audience, including financial professionals, technology enthusiasts, scholars, and policymakers who are keen to grasp the complexities and potentials of Fintech. As you journey through its chapters, you will gain insights into the adoption processes, the transformative power of AI and machine learning, the revolutionary potential of blockchain, and the critical role of big data and IoT in the digital age. Each chapter is designed to shed light on the opportunities these technologies present while also addressing the inherent risks and challenges they pose. By providing a balanced perspective, "Navigating the Fintech Frontier" seeks to equip readers with the knowledge needed to navigate the evolving landscape of financial services, fostering a deeper appreciation of both the promises and perils that come with embracing innovation in finance.

Abdul-Razak Abubakari
Entrepreneurship and Enterprise Development
Tamale Technical University, Tamale, Ghana

Mohammed Majeed
Marketing Department
Tamale Technical University, Tamale, Ghana

Nurideen Alhassan
Accountancy Department
Tamale Technical University, Tamale, Ghana

&

Jonas Yomboi
Accountancy Department
Valley View University
Oyibi-Ghana

List of Contributors

Abdul-Razak Abubakari Entrepreneurship and Enterprise Development, Tamale Technical University, Tamale, Ghana

Esther Asiedu Department of Management Studies, Business School, Ghana Communication Technology University, Ghana

Evans Kelvin Gyau Accountancy Department, Sunyani Technical University, Sunyani, Ghana

Jonas Yomboi Accountancy Department, Valley View University, Oyibi-Ghana

Jayadatta Shreepada Department of Marketing Management, KLE's Institute of Management Studies and Research (IMSR), BVB Campus, Vidyanagar, Hubli, Karnataka State, India

Mohammed Majeed Marketing Department, Tamale Technical University, Tamale, Ghana

Mohammad Irfan NSB Academy, Business School, Bengaluru, Karnataka 560099, India

Nurideen Alhassan Accountancy Department, Tamale Technical University, Tamale, Ghana

Victoria Manu Accountancy Department, Valley View University, Oyibi-Ghana

CHAPTER 1

Opportunities and Constraints of Fintech in Financial Services

Esther Asiedu[1,*]

[1] *Department of Management Studies, Business School, Ghana Communication Technology University, Ghana*

Abstract: Financial Technologies (Fintech) are used to define a number of new business models and technological advances that have the potential to alter the financial services sector. Hence, the goal of this chapter is to provide a complete overview of the new opportunities and potential constraints that FinTech presents to the financial services industry. Through FinTech, issuers, investors, and intermediaries interact, investigate, connect, share, engage, crowdsource, cooperate, and trade in methods that are fundamentally different from the past, ultimately disrupting the banking sector. The numerous barriers to FinTech include: compliance with anti-money laundering measures; market share competition (strategic risk); full trust; increasingly high expectations; regulatory; risks to the operation; security; and ethical questions.

Keywords: Barriers, Benefits, FinTech, Financial services, Technology.

INTRODUCTION

In the financial services business, "FinTech" refers to the application of technologies to enhance financial operations (Schueffel, 2016). Financial technology (FinTech) introduces a new paradigm in which information technology is fueling advancement in the financial sector. If FinTech is truly revolutionary, it will have a profound impact on traditional financial markets. Companies that provide cutting-edge financial technology are known as "FinTech," which is an acronym for "financial technology." Since 2010, there has been a considerable rise in the number of these businesses. It is not uncommon for FinTech companies to be tiny, micro, or medium-sized, but they have a clear vision of how to provide new or improve existing services in the financial services sector. It is predicted that FinTech will transform the financial services industry

* **Corresponding author Esther Asiedu:** Department of Management Studies, Business School, Ghana Communication Technology University, Ghana; E-mail: easaiedu011@gctu.edu.gh

Abdul-Razak Abubakari, Mohammed Majeed, Nurideen Alhassan and Jonas Yomboi (Eds.)

by reducing costs, enhancing service levels, and creating a more diverse and stable financial landscape. FinTech startups are able to displace traditional financial institutions by offering services that are distinct, specialized, and tailored to individual customers because of advances in infrastructure, big data, data analytics, and mobile devices (Lee & Shin, 2017). As a result of significant advancements in several disciplines (such as wireless networks and data analytics; user authentication; integrated mobile devices; data storage; picture recognition and data analytics), a broad variety of FinTech systems have been developed in various domains. FinTech has become a popular topic in the market because of a multitude of factors, including technological advancement, research and innovation expectations (market), cost-saving requirements, and consumer desires. The financial technology sector is also searching for help with improving individual funding requirements and industry groups' market performance (Hornuf *et al.*, 2020). This is why many successful financial institutions have made FinTech an essential part of their strategy. In addition, there is a paucity of research comparing the advantages and disadvantages of FinTech in other countries. Although FinTechs have been around for a long time, attention from a wide range of stakeholders has only just begun to focus on them (Arner *et al.* 2016). Consequently, research in this area is still in its infancy and progressing at a slow pace (Imam *et al.*, 2022). In both developed and emerging countries, the growth and spread of FinTechs are increasing (Arner *et al.* 2016; Patil *et al.* 2018). Therefore, the chapter's goal is to provide a complete overview of the new opportunities and potential constraints that FinTech presents to the financial services industry. FinTech stakeholders will benefit from extensive analyses of the potential issues, opportunities, and risks. In addition, it will provide greater opportunities for future research into FinTech areas that have not yet been investigated. These considerations serve as a foundation for the discussion that follows, which provides an in-depth look at how FinTech might benefit the banking industry while also highlighting the potential dangers and difficulties that may arise when integrating FinTech applications into existing systems.

LITERATURE

FinTech

Firms or representatives of firms that integrate financial services with cutting-edge technology are referred to as "FinTech" (Dorfleitner *et al.*, 2017). Innovative business concepts and emerging technology that could revolutionize the financial services industry are referred to as "FinTech," or Financial Technologies. A "technology-enabled innovation in financial services that could result in new business models, applications, procedures, or products with a related physical influence on the delivery of banking services" was defined by the Financial

Stability Board as FinTech (Financial Stability Board, 2017). Finance and investment, operations and risk management, payments, and infrastructure are just a few of the sectors in which FinTech is now focusing (Arner *et al.*, 2015). According to Stewart and Jürjens, FinTech can also be defined as the use of mobile devices or other digital platforms to access a bank account, receive transaction notifications, and receive debit and credit alerts through SMS or other electronic notifications. FinTech has grown from a small group of startups trying to take on and defeat established players to a much bigger ecosystem of enterprises willing to collaborate in many circumstances. FinTech firms require more than simply money; they also need clients. New techniques are needed to drive change and innovation among incumbents (PWC, 2017).

Benefits of FinTech

According to marketing literature, in the present era, educating clients about the benefits and procedures of using technical items will affect their decision to use them (Lewnes & Keller 2019). There is also a belief that a single technology product may not be able to penetrate the market in the current day and that collaborations and partnerships are necessary (Lewnes & Keller 2019). While it is important for FinTechs to deliver lower-cost and more convenient services, it is also important for providers to work together to market their services and educate end customers so that they may get the most out of the technology (Imam *et al.*, 2022). P2P and ECF platforms use this to provide credit to borrowers, particularly small and medium-sized enterprises (SMEs), who do not have easy access to bank loans (Peters & Panayi, 2016; Yomboi *et al.*, 2021). As a complement to traditional banking services, many bank executives around the world see FinTech as a way to "pump" new life into the system and bring it closer to the average customer. Through joint ventures, service outsourcing, or venture capital funding or acquisition, this might be accomplished. FinTechs appear to have a positive impact on these institutions rather than a negative one (Lines, 2016).

Because of the rise of FinTech solutions, financial institutions now have more options for improving their infrastructure and product lines (Jamil & Seman, 2019). Financial technology (FinTech) has the potential to boost operational effectiveness, enhance customer-centric services, and promote greater openness in the financial services industry. In order to lower borrowing costs, FinTech platforms can assist financial institutions in becoming more efficient (Mardiana and Kembauw 2021). As mentioned above, FinTechs can have far-reaching effects on financial services on a national scale. More hopeful about FinTech's significance in the financial service business, Loo (2018) believes that this revolution can positively impact financial service growth by decreasing financial crises' chances. Technology for Regulating Business (Regtech) FinTech innovations can assist financial organizations in meeting regulatory standards and accomplishing regulatory goals (such as prudential requirements, including reporting and consumer protection). More efficient approaches to improving compliance and risk management can be found in regTech, which can benefit banks. As the regulatory landscape evolves, this could be a way to adapt and reduce the costs of complying with the new rules (Peters & Panayi, 2016). FinTech development has the potential to increase employment, open up new business ventures, and bridge the digital divide, among other things (Zhang *et al.* 2020).

When FinTech is introduced into banking, Todorof (2018) believes that it can increase competitiveness and inclusion. In order to close the credit gap between countries, an increasing number of low-cost products and services would be needed. Banking services are more personalised and customised. FinTech firms' specialty is helping banks improve their traditional services in a way that is both economical and flexible. A white-labeled robo-advisory service could be offered by banks to assist their customers in navigating the investment world and deliver a more personalised service (Financial Stability Board, 2017). As an added bonus, banks and FinTech start-ups can work together to gain access to each other's customer bases as well as the world of global payment systems. FinTech enterprises will be able to enter the banking sector with fewer obstacles and acquire the trust of their clients as a result (Juengerkes, 2016).

Barriers of FinTech

Compliance with Anti-Money Laundering Measures

Laws and regulations aimed at preventing money laundering by unethical means are known as "anti-money laundering (AML) (Al-Ajlouni & Al-hakim, 2018). Those in the FinTech and money service industries who do not follow the rules risk fines, suspension, or revocation of their licenses, as well as damage to their brand's reputation. AML and KYC regulations for money service organisations are particularly difficult to comply with (Basel Committee on Banking Supervision, BCBS, 2017).

Market Share Competition (Strategic risk)

Individual banks face greater profitability concerns due to the fast unbundling of bank services to non-bank FinTech or BigTech enterprises. If new entrants are able to exploit innovation more effectively and produce lower-priced services that better satisfy client expectations, existing financial institutions could lose a significant portion of their market share or profit margin (BCBS, 2017; Financial Stability Board, 2017).

Full trust

It is been found that trust is the most important component in FinTech acceptance, according to Rossi and Utkus (2020). Using data from the Consumer Financial Protection Bureau, Bertsch *et al.* (2020) found a link between bank misconduct and online loan utilisation that was statistically significant. This research, in contrast to Bertsch *et al.* (2020), takes on the difficulty of examining potential endogeneity in the relationship between bank misbehaviour and FinTech lending and explores the role of trust in banks as an entry barrier for FinTech adoption. FinTech is believed to be an alternative transaction for the community since it facilitates access to financial products, simplifies transactions, and improves financial literacy (Wijayanti & Pradipta, 2017). However, despite the attention FinTech has received, its long-term usage is still under question. As a result of these concerns, some users are reluctant to continue using FinTech (Ryu, 2018).

Expectations are Increasing

As consumers become more savvy and knowledgeable about the world around them, they demand a higher level of personalisation and ease from their financial institutions. A major factor in these expectations is the changing demographics of banking clients. With each new generation of banking customers, there is an inherent grasp of technology and, as a result, a greater expectation of digital services (Wingard, 2022).

Regulatory

Increasingly severe standards and criteria are being imposed on banks as a result of government regulation. Market transparency necessitates that banks exhibit compliance and governance, as well as ensuring their safety when dealing with clients and other businesses. It has become a major problem for banks to maintain regulatory compliance because of the huge increase in regulatory fees relative to earnings and credit losses since the 2008 financial crisis. FinTech success depends on a clear-sighted assessment of regulatory risk since regulatory uncertainty makes business planning extremely difficult and the financial and compliance costs of regulation have been sufficient to force some new companies out of the market (Allen & Overy, 2017). The process of gaining trust in new FinTech services is a lengthy one. Adoption costs and early adopters may be affected by the regulatory environment, such as government-initiated cryptocurrency regulations in some countries (Luther 2016). When considering FinTech, governments must take into account the consequences of universal norms and legal principles to the extent that they align with national interests (Dong He *et al.*, 2017). Financial institutions are being forced to alter their business models because of the high cost of compliance management. The conventional sources of banking profitability are under stress as the cost of capital rises, interest rates remain low, return on equity declines, and proprietary trading declines. Despite this, the expectations of shareholders remain unaltered.

Risks to the Operation

It may become increasingly difficult to manage and control operational risk in financial services due to the development of innovative goods and services (BCBS, 2017). The emergence of FinTech creates greater IT interrelations between market participants (banks, FinTech, and others) and market infrastructures, which could lead to a systemic crisis if services are concentrated in a few dominant firms. Complexity in the banking industry has been increased by FinTech firms entering the market, which may have insufficient skills and experience in handling IT risks (Al-Ajlouni & Al-hakim, 2018).

Security

Customers' willingness to use FinTech services may suffer as a result of their growing apprehension about security breaches (Kang 2018).

An Ethical Question

Ethical concerns are one of the most common obstacles encountered while employing Big Data FinTech. Because of the various ways in which data and information can now be accessed, one persistent ethical issue is the issue of data privacy. Sharing personal information about individuals with a third party is immoral from an ethical standpoint; hence, protecting and securing the confidentiality of any data obtained from individuals is a must if data ethics are to be upheld.

CONCLUSION

Regardless of the fact that the finance sector and legislators around the world are paying attention to FinTech firms, little scientific research has been done on the topic yet. Accordingly, the purpose of this chapter is to identify the advantages and disadvantages of FinTech in the banking industry. Emerging technologies, such as blockchain and artificial intelligence, are helping to transform the financial services industry. By focusing on these technologies, incumbents will be able to move closer to FinTech, quickly react to the rapidly changing environment and regulations, and ultimately provide a better customer experience for consumers. Customers are becoming more empowered and/or in charge of their financial affairs through the digital solutions that banks are implementing. In the medium term, banks are likely to focus on improving their customer experience, even if this means that they miss out on transformational growth prospects and divert emphasis away from attaining projected performance. As a result, there are numerous obstacles to FinTech adoption in the banking sector. Such barriers to FinTech include: compliance with anti-money laundering measures; market share competition (strategic risk); full trust; increasing expectations ; regulatory; risks to the operation; and security and ethical questions.

To establish a secure and convenient solution, FinTech in financial services needs to be defined. Various mobile payment and security research are being undertaken in order to safely provide such mobile payment services. Due diligence checks, for example, can be automated to provide complete confidence in action. Due to fewer human errors, the use of automation can help businesses avoid fines and other consequences as a result of mistakes.

REFERENCES

African Business (2020). How can Africa monetise big data? *African Business*. Retrieved from: https://african.business/2020/12/technology-information/how-can-africa-monetise-big-data/.

Al-Ajlouni, A. T., & Al-hakim, M. (2018). Financial Technology in Banking Industry: Challenges and Opportunities. *Presented in the International Conference on Economics and Administrative Sciences ICEAS*.

Allen, & Overy. (2017). FinTech.

Ashraf, S.A., Javed, A.F., Bala, P.K. Barriers of fintech adoption in MSMEs: Moderating role of innovation culture. *ACIS 2021 Proceedings, 73*. Available from: https://aisel.aisnet.org/acis2021/73

Arner, D., Barberis, J., & Buckley, R. (2015). The Evolution of FinTech: A New Post-Crisis Paradigm. *UNSW Law Research Series Research Paper No. 2015/047*.
[http://dx.doi.org/10.2139/ssrn.2676553]

Basel Committee on Banking Supervision-BCBS, (2017). Sound Practices: Implications of fintech developments for banks and bank supervisors. BSI, Retrieved from Basel-Switzerland: Available from: https://www.bis.org/bcbs/publ/d415.htm.

He, D., Leckow, R., Haksar, V., Mancini-Griffoli, T., Jenkinson, N., M. K., Khiaonarong, T., & Rochon, C. H. T. (2017). *FinTech and financial services: Initial considerations*. IMF Staff Discussion Note, SDN/17/05. International Monetary Fund.

Financial Stability Board. (2019). *FinTech and market structure in financial services: Market developments and potential financial stability implications* (Report). Retrieved July 25, 2020, from: https://www.fsb.org/wp-content/ uploads/P140219.pdf.

Gomber, P., Kauffman, R.J., Parker, C., Weber, B.W. (2018). On the Fintech revolution: interpreting the forces of innovation, disruption, and transformation in financial services. *J. Manage. Inf. Syst., 35*(1), 220-265.
[http://dx.doi.org/10.1080/07421222.2018.1440766]

Hansen, T. (2012). Understanding trust in financial services the influence of financial healthiness, knowledge, and satisfaction. *J. Serv. Res., 15*(3), 280-295.
[http://dx.doi.org/10.1177/1094670512439105]

Juengerkes, B. E. (2016). FinTechs and Banks–Collaboration is Key. *The FinTech Book: The Financial Technology Handbook for Investors, Entrepreneurs and Visionaries,* 179-182.
[http://dx.doi.org/10.1002/9781119218906.ch47]

Jamil, N.N., Seman, J.A. (2019). The Impact of Fintech on the Sustainability of Islamic Accounting and

Finance Education in Malaysia. *Journal of Islamic Social Economics and Development, 4*(17), 74-88.

Imam, T., McInnes, A., Colombage, S., Grose, R. (2022). Opportunities and Barriers for FinTech in SAARC and ASEAN Countries. *J. Risk Financ. Manag., 15*(2), 77.
[http://dx.doi.org/10.3390/jrfm15020077]

Li, Y., Spigt, R., & Swinkels, L. (2017). The impact of FinTech start-ups on incumbent retail banks' share prices. *Financial Innovation, 3*(1), 1-16..
[http://dx.doi.org/10.1186/s40854-017-0076-7]

Kang, J. (2018). Mobile payment in Fintech environment: trends, security challenges, and services. *Human-centric Computing and Information Sciences, 8*(1), 32.
[http://dx.doi.org/10.1186/s13673-018-0155-4]

Leong, K., Sung, A. (2018). FinTech (Financial Technology): what is it and how to use technologies to create business value in fintech way? *Int. J. Innov. Manag. Technol., 9*(2), 74-78.
[http://dx.doi.org/10.18178/ijimt.2018.9.2.791]

Lewnes, A., Keller, K.L. (2019). 10 Principles of Modern Marketing. *MIT Sloan Manag. Rev., 60*, 1-10.

Loo, R.V. (2018). Making innovation more competitive: the case of Fintech. *UCLA Law Rev., 65*, 232.

Luther, W.J. (2016). Bitcoin and the Future of Digital Payments. *The Independent Review, 20*, 397-440.

Patil, P.P., Nripendra, P.R., Yogesh, K.D. (2018). Digital Payments Adoption Research: A Review of Factors Influencing Consumer's Attitude, Intention and Usage. In: Al-Sharhan, S.A., Simintiras, A.C., Dwivedi, Y.K., Janssen, M., Mäntymäki, M., Tahat, L., Moughrabi, I., Ali, T.M., Rana, N.P., (Eds.), *Challenges and Opportunities in the Digital Era I3E 2018.* (Vol. 11195, pp. 45-52). Cham: Springer International Publishing.
[http://dx.doi.org/10.1007/978-3-030-02131-3_6]

Pricewater house copers (2017). Redrawing the lines: FinTech's growing influence on Financial Services. *Global FinTech Report 2017.*

Priya, P.K., Kanagala, A. (2019). Fintech Issues and Challenges in India. *International Journal of Recent Technology and Engineering, 8*, 2277-3878.

Ryu, H.-S. (2018). What makes users willing or hesitant to use FinTech?: The moderating effect of user type. *Industrial Management & Data Systems.*
[http://dx.doi.org/10.1108/IMDS-07-2017-0325]

Saksonova, S., Kuzmina-Merlino, I. (2017). Fintech as Financial Innovation - The Possibilities and Problems of Implementation. *Eur. Res. Stud., XX*(3A), 961-973.
[http://dx.doi.org/10.35808/ersj/757]

Stewart, H., Jürjens, J. (2018). Data security and consumer trust in FinTech Innovation in Germany. *Information and Computer Security.*
[http://dx.doi.org/10.1108/ICS-06-2017-0039]

Schueffel P., (2016), Taming the Beast: A Scientific Definition of Fintech. *Institute of Finance*, pp. 1-24 Available from: https://ssrn.com/abstract=3097312.
[http://dx.doi.org/10.2139/ssrn.3097312]

Todorof, M. (2018). Shari'ah-compliant Fintech in the banking industry. *ERA Forum, 19*(1), 1-17.

Wijayanti, D. M., & Pradipta, H. (2017). Sharia FinTech: Positive Innovation in Consumer Perspective. Paper presented at the *International Seminar Academic Network on Competition Policy*, Bali.

Wingard, L. (2022). Top 10 Banking Industry Challenges — And How You Can Overcome Them. Hitachi Solutions. Available from: https://global.hitachi-solutions.com/.

Yomboi, J., Nangpiire, C., Kutochigaga, E.A., Majeed, M. (2021). The impact of the collapsed banks on customers in Ghana. *Asian Journal of Economics, Business and Accounting, 21*(17), 15-25.
[http://dx.doi.org/10.9734/ajeba/2021/v21i1730487]

Zetzsche, Dirk, Ross P. Buckley, Douglas W. Arner, and Janos N. Barberis, (2017). From fintech to techfin: The regulatory challenges of data-driven finance. *SSRN Electronic Journal.* Available from: https://papers.ssrn.com/sol3/papers.cfm?abstract_id=2959925. [http://dx.doi.org/10.2139/ssrn.2959925]

CHAPTER 2

The Theoretical Perspective of the Adoption of Fintech in the Financial Services Industry

Jonas Yomboi[1,*], Abdul-Razak Abubakari[2], Mohammed Majeed[3] and **Nurideen Alhassan[4]**

[1] *Accountancy Department, Valley View University, Oyibi-Ghana*

[2] *Entrepreneurship and Enterprise Development, Tamale Technical University, Tamale, Ghana*

[3] *Marketing Department, Tamale Technical University, Tamale, Ghana*

[4] *Accountancy Department, Tamale Technical University, Tamale, Ghana*

Abstract: This chapter aims to provide a comprehensive overview of the theoretical perspective of FinTech adoption in the financial services industry. By exploring factors influencing adoption and employing the Technology Acceptance Model (TAM), the study seeks to broaden understanding of the benefits and risks associated with FinTech adoption, aiding practitioners in developing strategies to enhance benefits and mitigate risks effectively. The study reveals several critical determinants influencing the adoption of FinTech in the banking industry. These include security concerns, perceived usefulness, perceived risk, social influence, self-efficacy, perceived ease of use, transaction costs, trust, and enabling conditions. Security concerns emerge as a significant barrier, alongside perceived risk, particularly regarding financial, legal, and security risks. However, perceived usefulness, ease of use, and social influence positively influence adoption intentions. Transaction costs and trust also play pivotal roles in shaping adoption decisions. Moreover, the study underscores the transformative potential of FinTech in reshaping the financial services landscape, emphasizing the need for collaborative efforts to maximize benefits while addressing associated challenges.

Keywords: Banking, Financial, Fintech, Industry, Legal, TAM.

INTRODUCTION

FinTechs (financial technologies) have expanded the financial services digital ecosystem across countries, particularly during the COVID-19 crisis (Abdillah 2020; Rahman *et al.*, 2018). However, FinTech adoption in different developing

* **Corresponding author Jonas Yomboi:** Accountancy Department, Valley View University, Oyibi-Ghana; E-mail: jonasyomboi@gmail.com

countries has been slow, despite them having different opportunities for growth and expansion of the digital economy, which is vital for future economic sustainability (Iman 2018; Zhang *et al.*, 2020). The influence that FinTech has on the market is growing and the long-term potential is even greater. Mainstream financial institutions are rapidly embracing the disruptive nature of FinTech and forging partnerships in efforts to sharpen operational efficiency and respond to customer demands for more innovative services (PWC, 2017). FinTech businesses have been at the forefront of the digital revolution in the financial sector, pushing traditional institutions to keep up. Unlike traditional institutions, FinTech companies are characterized as digital, agile and modern (Currencycloud, 2019).

The demand for digital financial services is all time high. Investment in FinTech start-ups is booming, reaching a record of $31 billion (£24 billion) in 2018, more than double that of the previous year (Currencycloud, 2019). FinTech money service businesses have fulfilled the need for easy, accessible, and affordable financial services and now play an integral role in the global economy. FinTech companies have even enabled new types of growth in the industry: collaborative disruption has enabled community banks to grow their customer base. In reality, the FinTech industry is still in its infancy, full of untapped potential, and growing every day (Currencycloud, 2019). FinTech enables banks to revamp their traditional brick-and-mortar business models into technologically revolutionized ones. Technologies like Big Data Analytics, Artificial Intelligence (AI), Machine learning, Blockchain, Crowdfunding, *etc.* are changing how banks operate today (Ebrahim & Abdulla, 2021). These technological and digital innovations can provide new business opportunities by transforming how financial institutions create value and deliver products and services. FinTech innovations in banks are expected to reach far beyond what most people think of online banking as a technological advancement in banks (Ebrahim & Abdulla, 2021). Despite the fact that FinTech players attract global attention from financial industry leaders and legislators, the issue as a subject of study is still in its infant stage, and little research has been conducted yet. Therefore, the purpose of the chapter is to provide a comprehensive overview of the theoretical perspective of the adoption of FinTech in the financial services industry. This study makes several contributions to the literature: First, new insights into the benefits and risks of Fintech adoption can be gained from this study. It is the goal of this chapter to broaden the definition of "continuous use" to include both positive and negative factors. To help practitioners better understand benefit and risk perceptions that may be used to build benefit-enhancing and risk-reducing strategies for Fintech adoption, this study employs the TAM framework. As our chapter shows, it is important for firms to know what factors to prioritise or avoid while providing Fintech to their banks.

LITERATURE

FinTech

The FinTech sector, in contrast to more traditional financial institutions, relies nearly completely on cutting-edge internet-based software to meet the demands of its customers (PwC 2016). FinTech is a term that describes the application of cutting-edge information technology, such as big data, cloud computing, and mobile computing, to enhance the quality and efficiency of financial services while also expanding their reach (Hu *et al.*, 2019). Finance, asset management, insurance, loyalty programs, payment, and regulatory technology are just a few of the nine categories of FinTech enterprises. Other categories include education and training (Keong, Leong & Bio, 2020).

The Adoption of FinTech in the Financial Services Industry

Financial technology-driven startups are challenging an industry that has witnessed little innovation in the past few decades, making traditional banking increasingly unappealing to the next generation. Newcomers in the financial industry are starting to take advantage of this technology to modernise financial services at a time when customers are losing faith in the stability and performance of traditional banks in the wake of the global financial crisis and increased monitoring and supervision of the banking industry. FinTech is described as the 21st century's answer to the banking industry, (Todorof, 2018). ICT's evolving involvement in financial services has allowed for completely new and creative financial solutions to be provided. Consumer behavior, ecosystems, and enabling legislation are all evolving, allowing the financial services industry to offer whole new, innovative financial solutions (Puschmann, 2017; KPMG, 2019). Financial technology (FinTech) may be coming to light in the financial sector, as seen by recent developments in the use of mobile applications and websites (Ebrahim & Abdulla, 2021). Using computer-based technology, FinTech has changed the financial services business. With the goal of making the financial industry more efficient, FinTech is generally referred to be digital innovation and financial services combined. FinTech, according to Zavolokina, Dolata, and Schwabe (2017), is a combination of technical innovation and finance that has the potential to revolutionise the financial services sector. In the FinTech market, consumers' expectations of performance, perceived benefits, utility, usability and related risks can impact their decision to utilise FinTech services (Keong, Leong & Bio, 2020).

Technology Acceptance Model (TAM)

Davis (1989) was the first to propose the use of TAM to measure users' internal views about IT adoption as a way to begin investigating the impact of technology adoption. When a new piece of technology has been accepted by users, the TAM model can help pinpoint the changes that need to be made before the system can be considered fully operational. Numerous studies have combined TAM with the adoption of other technologies, such as insurance customers' intent to use TAM, mobile banking, and credit card use, to use TAM as a measurement (Keong, Leong & Bio, 2020). TAM is one of the most well-known theoretical models. In 1975, Fishbein and Ajzen proposed the notion of rational action (Fishbein & Ajzen, 1975). Reasoned action is one prominent expansion of the concept of TAM. Davis suggested it in 1989, and it was used to explain the process of how people embrace and employ new technologies (Davis, 1989; Davis *et al.*, 1989). Acceptance of an information system is influenced by how valuable it is perceived and how user-friendly it is. Davis asserts that users' attitudes and intentions are influenced by their perceptions of the usefulness and ease of use of a product (Davis 1985). Models of sophisticated technology's application to everyday life, such as social networks, digital libraries, online banking, and mobile banking (Chen *et al.*, 2016), have been widely employed in a number of studies (Patel & Patel, 2018).

Determinants of FinTech Adoption

The purpose of this chapter is to look into the factors that influence the adoption of FinTech in the banking industry.

Security Concerns

The capability and commitment to keep confidential financial information secure during transmission and storage are regarded as security risks (Taherdoost, 2017). With the introduction of digital wallets and payment systems, the Fintech sector has grown at an exponential rate. The increasing adoption of technology and innovation by financial services firms has opened the door to an almost infinite number of possibilities for improving the customer experience. However, there are indisputable problems, and one of the most pressing concerns in the sector today is the security of financial technology (Taherdoost, 2018). Technology uptake, mobile payment use, and e-commerce acceptance have all been hindered by worries about security (Ogbanufe & Kim, 2018; Taherdoost, 2017).

Perceived Usefulness

The extent to which banks believe that employing technology, in this case FinTech and associated m-banking services, would help the firm is known as perceived usefulness (PU). FinTech can be viewed as a means of improving the user experience and financial competitiveness (Tang *et al.*, 2020). FinTech promotes customers by allowing them to obtain an environment of amplification and openness, minimise expenses, eliminate intermediaries, and make financial information more accessible (Zavolokina *et al.*, 2016). Economic benefits, ease, and transaction procedures are the three key elements of perceived benefits identified by Ryu (2018). "A customer's sense of the possibility for FinTech adoption to result in a positive outcome," is defined by the author as perceived benefits. The findings of this study suggest that perceived benefits influence FinTech adoption positively. FinTech can reduce transaction and capital costs compared to traditional financial services, allowing FinTech consumers to benefit financially. FinTech adoption, according to Carlin *et al.* (2017), minimises financial fee payments and penalties.

Perceived Risk

Consumers' perceptions of risk play a role in influencing whether or not new technologies are adopted. The idea of perceived risk is utilised to understand consumer behavior, as Tang *et al.* (2020) emphasize. In FinTech contexts in Africa, identity theft, phishing, hacking, malware, data breaches, and SIM swaps are frequent. In the financial services industry, new ideas are always accompanied by significant risks (Kim *et al.*, 2008; Ryu, 2018). PR surrounding the usage of FinTech is seen as a significant impediment to technological adoption (Ryu 2018). Customers' perception of risk influences their desire to use FinTech services: financial risk, legal risk, and activity risk are all major influencers, whereas security risk has no substantial effect on customers' desire to use FinTech services (Tang *et al.*, 2020). In FinTech, PR refers to the uncertainty that customers feel about FinTech and the possible negative consequences of using it (Ryu 2018). It is essential to create user trust in the early stages of m-banking adoption because of the high levels of security risk and cheap switching costs (Slazus & Bick, 2022). In case of FinTech adoption, perceived risk is also a significant determinant. According to Wu and Wang (2005), consumers' willingness to use mobile payments is strongly correlated with their assessment of the risk involved. A study by Li *et al.* (2020) found that those who are more willing to take risks will be more likely to use mobile payment systems. Perceived financial, legal, security, and operational risks were all examined by Ryu in 2018. Perceived risk significantly impacts FinTech adoption, while legal risks have the biggest negative impact. (Ryu, 2018).

Social Influence

Venkatesh *et al.* (2003) defined social influence as the extent to which an individual believes that influential others think they should use a new system. Banks are adopting FinTech because they believe that their clients will accept and utilise new solutions. People in the surrounding environment can have a significant impact on a person's conduct. The same is true for organisations in the same sector that play a role in promoting the use of FinTech solutions. Studies of m-banking adoption have found a correlation between social influence and m-banking usage intentions (Maduku, 2017; Makanyeza, 2017). It is common for customers to be influenced by other people's ideas when they utilise new technology, especially in the social media era, where they are more likely to be influenced by the thoughts of those around them. People are more likely to adopt new technologies if their loved ones, friends, and coworkers recommend them(Beldad & Hegner 2018). Because of this, SI is defined in this study as a person's critical opinion of others who believe the person should be using MFS platforms (*e.g.*, friends, family, relatives, and coworkers).

Self-efficacy

Researchers claimed that a user has achieved self-efficacy if they are able to do a task using new technology without the support of others (Compeau & Higgins, 1995). Employees who are unable to use FinTech because of a lack of availability or ease of use of SE will find themselves unable to advance in their positions. Consumers in underdeveloped nations are reluctant to use Internet banking because they lack confidence in their ability to do so, according to Alalwan *et al.* (2015). Self-efficacy, according to Wood and Albert, is the belief in one's ability to mobilise the motivation, cognitive resources, and course of action needed to meet certain situational demands (Wood and Bandura, 1989).

Perceived Ease of Use

A study of research has indicated that PEOU has a considerable impact on attitudes toward utilising FinTech and m-banking (Slazus & Bick, 2022, Wentzel *et al.*, 2013; Pandaya & Gupta, 2015; Singh & Srivastava, 2018). Customers are more inclined to use mobile banking if it is simple and straightforward for them to use (Dapp, 2014; Pandiya & Gupta, 2015).

Transaction Cost

Because of the technological transformation in banking, the provision of financial services may now be disaggregated, which has resulted in new business models and new entrants (Feyen *et al.*, 2021). Digital financial services can be more widely available and more people can benefit from them if transaction costs are reduced (Bachas *et al.*, 2018). Payments made easier by putting services closer to customers have resulted in increased customer satisfaction, which has boosted the performance of banks (Aduda & Kingoo, 2012).

Trust

Institutions rely on customers' faith and confidence in the security of their transactions to retain their customers' trust and confidence (Wentzel *et al.* 2013). According to Dapp (2014) and Zhou (2011), FinTech firms that can provide customers with long-term and reliable assurances of data security will have the most potential for growth and profitability. A successful FinTech company relies heavily on data protection, account safety, transparency, and clear communication in order to develop confidence and encourage customer adoption (Slazus & Bick, 2022). It is essential to create user trust in the early stages of m-banking adoption because of the significant security concerns and cheap switching costs (Singh & Srivastava, 2018; Zhou, 2011). They suggest that trust is a significant aspect not included in TAM; they believe trust could positively affect the adoption and experience of mobile payments since customers prefer to use mobile payment providers that they feel to be trustworthy and who have a proven track record of reliability. Customers' payment patterns have an impact on their level of trust.

Enabling Conditions

The degree to which an individual bank believes that FinTech organisations and technical infrastructure exist to facilitate system use is characterised as the "facilitating condition" (Venkatesh *et al.*, 2003). Organizations that have access to modern technology facilities are believed to have a competitive advantage since they are able to uncover and use customer information while cultivating long-term, one-to-one connections that are financially rewarding.

Benefits of FinTech

ICT advances in the last several years have enabled a slew of new financial services for consumers (Gomber *et al.*, 2018; Puschmann, 2017). In the future, mobile financial transactions may be made more accessible, cost-effective, and transparent through FinTech applications (Kim *et al.*, 2015). Because of its demonstrated capacity to remove investment barriers, financial technology (FinTech) has been widely adopted across markets worldwide (Hong *et al.*, 2020). However, the adoption of FinTech in established and developing economies is different (Frost, 2020). A study by Flood *et al.* (2013) expands the topic of the benefits of FinTech by looking at the social impact on FinTech users. As a result of FinTech, financial transactions have become more economical, convenient, and secure (Chen *et al.*, 2019; Puschmann, 2017). FinTech offers numerous advantages to customers, the most important of which is a reduction in the amount of time, effort, and money required to complete financial transactions (Ryu, 2018). "A user's view of the potential that FinTech use will result in a beneficial outcome" is the definition of perceived benefits (Ryu, 2018). COVID-19 has increased the use of technology in nearly every part of the world (Al Nawayseh 2020; Khatun *et al.* 2021). Digital banking adoption has increased by 3 to 10 years, according to financial experts (Reich 2021).

Fintech's most common and constant extrinsic motivator is its economic benefit to society (Kuo-Chuen & Teo, 2015). Financial technology (Fintech) transactions have the potential to lower costs while also generating profits. Mobile remittance and peer-to-peer lending are examples of Fintech apps that can minimise transaction costs for users by directly providing standardised services over a mobile channel without the need for intermediation (Mackenzie, 2015). A user's perception of advantages can be a good indicator of how useful FinTech applications are (Puschmann, 2017). Customers' willingness to use systems is influenced by their perceptions of their utility and ease of use (Ryu, 2018). As a result, several studies show that customers' intentions to adopt FinTech apps like mobile payment and Bitcoin can be positively influenced by perceived benefits (Stewart & Jürjens, 2018).

Future of FinTech

Blockchain, cloud computing, artificial intelligence (AI), and big data have all revolutionised the role of ICT in the FinTech business in terms of new opportunities, legal problems, and threats to the industry's integrity (Puschmann, 2017). Fintech is also characterised by the growing and strengthening role of IT. Due to advancements in traditional electronic financial services, Fintech has emerged as a cutting-edge method of providing financial services (Arner *et al.*, 2015). Financial and investment aspects, payments and infrastructure, operations and risk mitigation, data protection and monetization, as well as consumer interaction, are the primary areas of FinTech applications (Chen, Wu, & Yang, 2019). P2P lending, mobile payments, artificial intelligence and machine learning, digital advice and trading platforms, cryptocurrencies, and the blockchain are just some of the FinTech developments currently dominating. An issue for banks is how to keep up with the rapid technical advancements occurring in the FinTech industry. FinTech investments and acquisitions by banks are being made in order to remain competitive and maintain a larger market share in the financial industry. Reducing the financial risks that could arise in the industry requires collaboration between regulators, established banks, and FinTech startups. Increasing the potential advantages of FinTech products while minimising their possible risks is a huge issue for FinTech companies in this context. FinTech has received a fair amount of attention in the financial industry, but many individuals remain sceptical about its long-term application in Africa because of the significant dangers it entails. Improved transparency, lower costs, the elimination of middlemen, and faster access to financial information are just some of the benefits of FinTech.

CONCLUSION

Financial technology (FinTech) innovation is undergoing a dynamic and systemic shift around the world. There is, however, a dearth of information on how FinTech is perceived by actual customers. Changes in information technology have the ability to decouple and restructure existing financial services through FinTech. Using mobile, social networking sites, and the internet, FinTech enables customers to access banking services rather than relying on traditional methods such as over-the-counter transactions and teller machines, which are becoming increasingly obsolete. This chapter's implications for market behaviors, particularly in relation to financial institutions, can assist in banking analytical decisions. In addition, researchers can further enhance the research framework and retailer managers have identified the most important aspects that influence the acceptance of financial technologies like e-wallets. FinTech and TAM do have some generalizability, according to the literature.

REFERENCES

Al nawayseh, M.K. (2020). Fintech in COVID-19 and beyond: what factors are affecting customers' choice of fntech applications? *J. Open Innov., 6*(4), 153.
[http://dx.doi.org/10.3390/joitmc6040153]

Alalwan, A.A., Dwivedi, Y.K., Rana, N.P., Lal, B., Williams, M.D. (2015). Consumer adoption of Internet banking in Jordan: Examining the role of hedonic motivation, habit, self-efficacy and trust. *J. Financ. Serv. Mark., 20*(2), 145-157.
[http://dx.doi.org/10.1057/fsm.2015.5]

Arner, D.W., Barberis, J.N., Buckley, R.P. (2015). *The Evolution of Fintech: A New Post-Crisis Paradigm?* (pp. 1-46). Hong Kong: University of Hong Kong.

Beldad, A.D., Hegner, S.M. (2018). Expanding the technology acceptance model with the inclusion of trust, social infuence, and health valuation to determine the predictors of german users' willingness to continue using a ftness app: a structural equation modeling approach. *Int. J. Hum. Comput. Interact., 34*(9), 882-893.
[http://dx.doi.org/10.1080/10447318.2017.1403220]

Carlin, B., Olafsson, A., Pagel, M. (2017). Fintech Adoption across Generations: Financial Fitness in the Information Age (NBER Working Paper No. 23798). *Cambridge, MA: National Bureau of Economic Research.*
[http://dx.doi.org/10.3386/w23798]

Chen, M.A., Wu, Q., Yang, B. (2019). How valuable is FinTech innovation? *Rev. Financ. Stud., 32*(5), 2062-2106.
[http://dx.doi.org/10.1093/rfs/hhy130]

Chen, J-F., Chang, J-F., Kao, C-W., Huang, Y-M. (2016). *Integrating ISSM into TAM to Enhance Digital Library Services: A Case Study of the Taiwan Digital Meta-Library..* Taiwan: The Electronic Library.
[http://dx.doi.org/10.1108/EL-01-2014-0016]

Currencycloud (2019). Four Challenges Facing FinTech Businesses around the World. Available from: https://blog.currencycloud.com/.

Das, A., Das, D. (2020). Perception, Adoption, and Pattern of Usage of FinTech Services by Bank Customers: Evidences from Hojai District of Assam. *Emerging Economy Studies,* 6(1), 7-22. [http://dx.doi.org/10.1177/2394901520907728]

Davis, F. D. (1985). A technology acceptance model for empirically testing new end-user information systems: Theory and results (Doctoral dissertation). *Massachusetts Institute of Technology, Cambridge,* 2020, Available from: https://dspace.mit.edu/ handle/1721.1/15192.

Davis, F.D. (1989). Perceived Usefulness, Perceived Ease of Use, and User Acceptance of Information Technology. *Manage. Inf. Syst. Q.,* 13(3), 319-340. [http://dx.doi.org/10.2307/249008]

Ebrahim, R., Abdulla, Y. (2021). FinTech in banks: Opportunities and Challenges. Edited by Al-Bastaki, Y. Razzaque, A. and Sarea, A. (2021). *Innovative Strategies for Implementing FinTech in Banking.* [http://dx.doi.org/10.4018/978-1-7998-3257-7]

Dapp, T. (2014). *Fintech – The digital (r)evolution in the financial sector.* Frankfurt am Main, Germany: DB Research.

Financial Stability Board. (2019). FinTech and market structure in financial services: *Market developments and potential financial stability implications* (Report). Available from: https://www.fsb.org/wp-content/ uploads/P140219.pdf.

Gomber, P., Kauffman, R.J., Parker, C., Weber, B.W. (2018). On the Fintech revolution: Interpreting the forces of innovation, disruption, and transformation in financial services. *J. Manage. Inf. Syst.,* 35(1), 220-265. [http://dx.doi.org/10.1080/07421222.2018.1440766]

Kim, Y., Choi, J., Park, Y.J., Yeon, J.L. (2016). The adoption of mobile payment services for "fintech.". *Int. J. Appl. Eng. Res.,* 11(2), 1058-1061.

Kim, Y., Youngju, P., Jeongil, C., Jiyoung, Y. (2015). An Empirical Study on the Adoption of "Fintech" Service: Focused on Mobile Payment Services. *Ibusiness,* 136-140.

KPMG (2019). *The Pulse of Fintech 2019—Biannual Global Analysis of Investment in Fintech; KPMG:* Zurich, Switzerland, p. 80.

Tang, K.L., Ooi, C.K., Chong, J.B. (2020). Perceived Risk Factors Affect Intention To Use FinTech. *Journal of Accounting and Finance in Emerging Economies,* 6(2), 453-463. [http://dx.doi.org/10.26710/jafee.v6i2.1101]

Kuo-Chuen, D.L., Teo, E.G. (2015). Emergence of FinTech and the LASIC principles. *Journal of Financial Perspectives,* 3(3), 24-36.

Hu, Z., Ding, S., Li, S., Chen, L., Yang, S. (2019). Adoption Intention of Fintech Services for Bank Users: An Empirical Examination with an Extended Technology Acceptance Model. *Symmetry (Basel),* 11(3), 340. [http://dx.doi.org/10.3390/sym11030340]

Priya, R., Gandhi, A.V., Shaikh, A. (2018). Mobile banking adoption in an emerging economy. *Benchmarking (Bradf.),* 25(2), 743-762. [http://dx.doi.org/10.1108/BIJ-01-2016-0009]

Puschmann, T. (2017). Fintech. *Bus. Inf. Syst. Eng.,* 59(1), 69-76. [http://dx.doi.org/10.1007/s12599-017-0464-6]

Patel, K.J., Patel, H.J. (2018). Adoption of internet banking services in Gujarat. *Int. J. Bank Mark.,* 36(1), 147-169. [http://dx.doi.org/10.1108/IJBM-08-2016-0104]

PwC. (2017). Global Fintech Report. Available from: https://www.pwc.com/jg/en/publications/pwc-globa- -fintech-report-17.3.17-final.pdf (Accessed 10 Apr. 2018). .

Ryu, H. S. (2018). Understanding benefit and risk framework of FinTech adoption: Comparison of early adopters and late adopters. In *Proceedings of the 51st Hawaii International Conference on System Sciences*, 3864–3873. Waikoloa Village, Hawaii. Retrieved from: https://scholarspace.manoa.hawaii.edu.

Rahman Z (2020) As MFS grows, its regulations need to change. *The Business Standard*. Available from: https://www.tbsnews.net/thoughts/mfsgrows-its-regulations-need-change-136069 (Accessed 24 June 2021).

Reich, G. (2021). Online and mobile banking adoption soars, setting new benchmarks for 2021. *The Financial Brand*. Retrieved from: https://financialbrand.com/107582/garret-online-mobile-banking-adoption-rates-covid/.

Ryu, H.S. (2018). What makes users willing or hesitant to use Fintech?: the moderating effect of user type. *Ind. Manage. Data Syst., 118*(3), 541-569.
[http://dx.doi.org/10.1108/IMDS-07-2017-0325]

Stewart, H., Jürjens, J. (2018). Data security and consumer trust in FinTech innovation in Germany. *Inf. Comput. Secur., 26*(1), 109-128.
[http://dx.doi.org/10.1108/ICS-06-2017-0039]

Singh, S., Srivastava, R.K. (2018). Predicting the intention to use mobile banking in India. *Int. J. Bank Mark., 36*(2), 357-378.
[http://dx.doi.org/10.1108/IJBM-12-2016-0186]

Tang, K.L., Ooi, C.K., Chong, J.B. (2020). Perceived Risk Factors Affect Intention To Use FinTech. *Journal of Accounting and Finance in Emerging Economies, 6*(2), 453-463.
[http://dx.doi.org/10.26710/jafee.v6i2.1101]

Todorof, M. (2018). Shari'ah-compliant Fintech in the banking industry. *ERA Forum, 19*(1), 1–17.

Venkatesh, V., Morris, M.G., Davis, G.B., Davis, F.D. (2003). User acceptance of information technology: toward a unified view. Source. *Manage. Inf. Syst. Q., 27*(3), 425-478.
[http://dx.doi.org/10.2307/30036540]

Wang, Y.S., Lin, H.H., Luarn, P. (2006). Predicting consumer intention to use mobile service. *Inf. Syst. J., 16*(2), 157-179.
[http://dx.doi.org/10.1111/j.1365-2575.2006.00213.x]

Wentzel, J. P., Diatha, K. S., Yadavalli, V. (2013). An application of the extended technology acceptance model in understanding technology-enabled financial service adoption in South Africa. *Development Southern Africa, 30*(4-5), 659-673.

Wood, R., Bandura, A. (1989). Impact of conceptions of ability on self-regulatory mechanisms and complex decision making. *J. Pers. Soc. Psychol., 56*(3), 407-415.
[http://dx.doi.org/10.1037/0022-3514.56.3.407] [PMID: 2926637]

World Bank. (2016). Ghana - *Financial Inclusion Insights Survey 2014*. Retrieved from: https://microdata.worldbank.org/index.php/catalog/2730/related-materials.

Zhou, T. (2011). An empirical examination of initial trust in mobile banking. *Internet Res., 21*(5), 527-540.
[http://dx.doi.org/10.1108/10662241111176353]

CHAPTER 3

Risk Factors Affecting Customer Adoption of Fintech in the Financial Services Sector

Esther Asiedu[1,*]

[1] *Department of Management Studies, Business School, Ghana Communication Technology University, Ghana*

Abstract: This chapter delves into the complex landscape of Fintech services, highlighting both their transformative potential and the perceived risks that hamper widespread adoption. The chapter aims to bridge the knowledge gap in perceived risks and offers strategic guidance for banks and Fintech companies to mitigate these concerns, fostering safer and more effective integration of Fintech solutions into the financial ecosystem. The findings revealed that Fintech innovations like P2P lending, crowdsourcing, and blockchain have increased transparency, reduced costs, and facilitated greater accessibility of financial information. However, the study identifies significant concerns, including financial, legal, security, operational, and product-related risks, which influence consumer reluctance. Employing the theory of reasoned action, the chapter analyzes both the benefits and risks associated with Fintech, providing insights into why consumers might hesitate to adopt these technologies.

Keywords: Adoption, Customer, Fintech, Financial, Risk, Sector.

INTRODUCTION

Fintech services, or financial technology as a service, have gotten a lot of attention recently. FinTech companies' use of mobile technology has the unintended consequence of undermining consumer confidence and preventing the widespread adoption of this type of technology-driven business model. Using electronic channels to ease full loan transactions (Yuwei, Zhihan, and Bin, 2017), P2P lending, crowdsourcing, and invoice funding are examples of FinTech credit (Lenz, 2016). (Lenz, 2016; Suryono, Purwandaria, & Budia, 2019). Scholars and practitioners believe Fintech can have a transformative effect on banking, but some remain cautious because of the significant dangers involved. Fintech acceptance decisions are influenced by both positive and negative elements; therefore, we must learn more about why people are willing or unwilling to utilise

---

[*] **Corresponding author Esther Asiedu:** Department of Management Studies, Business School, Ghana Communication Technology University, Ghana; E-mail: easaiedu011@gctu.edu.gh

Abdul-Razak Abubakari, Mohammed Majeed, Nurideen Alhassan and Jonas Yomboi (Eds.)

it. An approach to benefit-risk analysis based on the theory of reasoned action has been proposed, which incorporates both the positives and the negatives of its adoption.

FinTech has the ability to create an environment of amplification and openness, lower costs, eliminate intermediaries, and make financial information more accessible to customers (Zavolokina, Dolata, & Schwabe, 2016). Consumers and financial service providers alike have reaped many benefits from fintech, but it is not without danger. There are both advantages and disadvantages to the financial ecosystem's disruption, which must be addressed by minimizing the risks and enhancing the advantages (Razzaque *et al.*, 2020; Wang *et al.*, 2020). In addition, it has been stated that comfort or simplicity of use, which are Fintech's major benefits, will always impact a user's attitude toward its use regardless of the perceived hazards of Fintech (Meyliana *et al.*, 2019). Fintechs allow customers to connect through a variety of mobile services, including making payments, transferring money, seeking loans, buying insurance, managing assets, and making investments (Ryu, 2018). According to Ryu's definition, "innovation and disruptive services are supplied by non-financial enterprises, where IT is the major aspect," and we'll use that description in this article as a starting point for defining "fintechs."

About 82% of financial institutions surveyed by Padmanaban and Soo (2016) were concerned about the threat that FinTech posed. Consumers are also concerned about the perceived dangers of using financial technology. FinTech development is widely accepted around the world, according to research. However, there is still a lack of clarity regarding the perceived risk factors that discourage users from utilising FinTech. Perceived risk in the use of FinTech is understudied (Keong, Leong, & Bao, 2020). As a result, the goal of this chapter is to close the perceived risk gap in the FinTech industry.

The chapter contributes to the literature as follows: it provides banks with information on how to prepare for the disruption of FinTech; hence, practitioners can better comprehend and remove risk barriers. The chapter also provides that FinTech's operational abilities and system functional performance should also be taken into consideration by bank managers.

LITERATURE

FinTech

Blockchain, machine intelligence, and 5G are just a few of the latest examples of cutting-edge technology that have begun to permeate the world of banking in recent years (Deng *et al.*, 2021). "Fintech" is an acronym for financial technology, which includes both financial services and information technology (IT) (or industries). The term "fintech" is defined in a variety of ways in academic writings. Fintech is defined by researchers such as Ryu (2018) and Kuo and Teo (2015) as financial service goods or services that were developed using highly innovative and disruptive service technologies. Some scholars believe that the emergence of Fintech will affect the business model of financial institutions and boost the risk-taking behaviour of commercial banks (Deng *et al.*, 2021). To highlight the financial system's weakness, Fintech encourages the formation of shadow banks through regulatory arbitrage and technical benefits (Buchak *et al.* 2018). Financial technology (Fintech) has the potential to bring about huge transformations, but it will also bring about considerable perceived risk challenges (Philippon, 2015), such as financial, security, legal/regulatory, operational, and product-related. All countries are actively investigating their own regulatory procedures in light of the rapid advancement of financial technology and associated threats.

Key Risk Factors for the Use of FinTech by Bank Customers

The acceptance of Fintech is still uncertain, despite the fact that many experts and practitioners believe it can transform the future of the financial industry. Because of the high risk involved, some people are reluctant to use Fintech. FinTech users are reluctant to adopt it because of the perceived risks they face. According to the researchers, there is a significant amount of ambiguity surrounding the outcomes of using new technologies (Tan & Leby, 2016; Farah, 2017; Ryu & Ko, 2020). In the realm of financial technology, scholars have identified a number of hazards that function as barriers for financial institutions, such as financial, legal, security, and operational risks. The following four types of risks were established as perceived risk factors when the Cunningham (1967) paradigm was transferred to the Fintech context: One of the most important aspects of a company's risk management strategy is to identify and mitigate financial, legal, and operational risks.

Financial Risk

In FinTech, the term "financial risk" refers to the possibility of financial losses (Ryu, 2018). Among the reasons given by Ryu (2018) for FinTech's financial losses is the risk of the budgetary exchange framework and currency misrepresentation, as well as the moral danger and the risk of additional exchange fees linked with preferred value. Finance-related losses are negatively associated with the intention to use fintech for a long time (World Economic Forum 2015; Zavolokina *et al.* 2016 b) because of the poor functioning of the system of financial transactions, financial fraud, moral risk, and additional transaction costs involved with the value of rapid adoption. There has been an increase in financial hazards in financial services, including the probability of fraud recurrence, according to Luo and colleagues (2010). An operating budget might also be disrupted by a company's financial service provider taking financial risks. According to Khalil and Alam (2020), an example of a financial loss is when the process of releasing a Fintech service takes longer than intended, therefore increasing the total cost of implementation. Digital technology used by Fintech is increasing the risk of financial losses owing to e-fraud (financial losses caused by electronic fraud) (Keong *et al.*, 2020).

Legal Risk

Uncertainty over FinTech's legal standing and a lack of adequate laws are examples of legal risk (Diana & Leon, 2020). Fintech's lack of clear legal status and thorough guidelines is a legal danger (Keong *et al.*, 2020). Financial technology (FinTech) is a new entrant to the market, so there are not any instructions on how to avoid monetary disasters and security difficulties. Legal risk refers to the danger that a financial institution would deviate from industry norms of operation or legal and regulatory requirements, resulting in legal action and a monetary penalty (Khalil & Alam, 2020). Financial losses or security breaches can cause users to be anxious or distrustful because there is no precedent for fintech businesses in the market (Ryu, 2018). The legal risk in the FinTech context relates to FinTech's uncertain legal status and lack of universal regulation. Customers' data and privacy, as well as the security of the financial system, are all examples of legal risk (Diana & Leon, 2020). Furthermore, Yuan and Xu (2020) noted that, despite the fact that Fintech was created to revolutionise the financial industry, regulatory rules would play a significant role in the risk governance of Fintech, which could limit the extent and degree of Fintech innovation. When it comes to competitive advantage, the technology giant known as "Big Technology" enters the banking industry, which has reduced bank profit margins and increased the banks' risk-taking level. A comprehensive legislative structure for effective control of the many hazards connected with Fintech innovation, as proposed by Yuan and Xu (2020), is needed to achieve a proper balance between technical innovation and risk prevention and enable the healthy development of Fintech.

Security Risk

When it comes to the security of FinTech financial transactions, consumers are particularly concerned about the possibility of losing money due to fraud or hacking, which is viewed as a violation of their privacy (Diana & Leon, 2020; Barakat & Hussainey, 2013; Charles *et al.*, 2023). It is important to understand that FinTech faces legal risk because there are no clear rules in place for the industry. Blackmailers or hacker attacks on a FinTech company's security system pose a significant security concern because of the potential misfortune that could be caused. The principle of security risk can be used to defend against attacks on electronic services. Consumers are most concerned about this (Lwin, Wirtz, & Williams, 2007). As a result of Fintech use, there is a risk of a significant loss of privacy, personal data, and transactions (Schierz *et al.*, 2010). Users' finances can be jeopardised by fraud and network infiltration, not to mention a lack of concern for their security (Ryu, 2018). Fintech security risk is directly linked to the dangers associated with digital technology because of the substantial deployment of digital components in Fintech solutions and platforms. Violations of digital security such as hacking, phishing, virus attacks, and e-fraud can all take advantage of flaws in digital systems to activate a crystallisation of risk. However, research has shown that the perceived danger of using Fintech solutions is not a substantial deterrent (Alao, 2020).

Operational Risk

Users face an operational risk that relates to future risks caused by system failures in the firm's internal systems, which are caused by the poor quality of FinTech systems and the workers who manage the organisation (Diana & Leon, 2020). Operations risk in FinTech is the potential loss resulting from internal flaws, people, or frameworks (Barakat & Hussainey, 2013). According to the Basel II framework of operational risk (OR) definition (Alao, 2020), people, processes, and systems make up the three dimensions of operational risk (OR) in the context of Fintech. In the wake of a number of high-profile operational failures affecting significant financial institutions, people are concerned about operational risk. In the FinTech environment, operational risk refers to the possible misfortune caused by defects or failures in internal processes, personnel, and frameworks, according to Keong and colleagues (2020). Users will stop using fintech if the bank's business systems and activities have high-risk possibilities. Users will be distrustful and dissatisfied with fintechs if their systems do not work well and their internal processes are inefficient, which will lead to a decrease in the number of people using them (Diana & Leon, 2020). As a result of risk crystallization, threats and vulnerabilities are more easily applicable to a business. Losses resulting from unsuccessful or inefficient products, services, processes, systems, people, and business models can be caused by both internal and external factors. This is the definition of "operational risk" (Alao, 2020; Khalil & Alam, 2020; Razzaque *et al.*, 2020).

Product Risk

Customers who lack the necessary knowledge and expertise may be exposed to larger risks of harm as a result of unsuitable financial products being made available to them. Product appropriateness and product design obligations could be imposed on fintech operators as possible remedies for less-aware consumers (Boeddub & Istuk, 2021). Because of this, financial transactions would be safe if Fintech solution providers could manufacture financial products and services in an operational environment that was devoid of threats and vulnerabilities.

CONCLUSION

This chapter's purpose was to explain why customers are reluctant to use an emerging financial service and to identify different risk perceptions. This chapter's literature adequately demonstrates the main hazards of Fintech adoption. Financial services and banking have been transformed in parts of emerging markets like Nigeria as a result of the introduction of financial technology. Fintech is increasingly being integrated into traditional banks' digital business strategies as they strive to go digital themselves. Despite the fact that Fintech adoption has been widely accepted by financial customers, there remain inherent hazards. This study gives bank/Fintech managers a better understanding of the factors they should focus on or avoid when selling Fintech services to their consumers. According to the research reviewed above, behavioural intentions to use Fintech in the banking industry are strongly influenced by perceptions of risk.

REFERENCES

Alao, B. (2020). An Appraisal of Potential Risks of Fintech Adoption in the Nigerian Financial Services Industry. *LIGS University.* Available from: https://ligsuniversity.com/blog/.

Barakat, A., Hussainey, K. (2013). Bank governance, regulation, supervision, and risk reporting: Evidence from operational risk disclosures in European banks. *Int. Rev. Financ. Anal., 30,* 254-273.
[http://dx.doi.org/10.1016/j.irfa.2013.07.002]

Boeddu, G., Chein, J., & Istuk, I. (2021). Addressing consumer risks in fintech to maximize its benefits. *World Bank Blogs.* Available from: https://blogs.worldbank.org/.

Buchak, G., Matvos, G., Piskorski, T., Seru, A. (2018). Fintech, regulatory arbitrage, and the rise of shadow banks. *J. Financ. Econ., 130*(3), 453-483.
[http://dx.doi.org/10.1016/j.jfineco.2018.03.011]

Charles, A., Yomboi, J., Arko-Cole, N., Tijani, A. (2023). Emerging Use of Technologies in Education. *Digital Transformation in Education: Emerging Markets and Opportunities. 82.*

Deng, L., Lv, Y., Liu, Y., Zhao, Y. (2021). Impact of Fintech on Bank Risk-Taking: Evidence from China. *Risks, 9*(5), 99.
[http://dx.doi.org/10.3390/risks9050099]

Diana, N., Leon, F.M. (2020). Factors Affecting Continuance Intention of FinTech Payment among Millennials in Jakarta. *European Journal of Business and Management Research, 5*(4).
[http://dx.doi.org/10.24018/ejbmr.2020.5.4.444]

Tang, K.L., Ooi, C.K., Chong, J.B. (2020). Perceived Risk Factors Affect Intention To Use FinTech. *Journal of Accounting and Finance in Emerging Economies, 6*(2), 453-463.
[http://dx.doi.org/10.26710/jafee.v6i2.1101]

Khalil, F., Alam, H.M. Identification of Fintech Driven Operational Risk Events. *Journal of the Research Society of Pakistan, 1*(57), 75-87. Available from: http://pu.edu.pk/images/journal/history/PDF-FILES/6_57_1_20.pdf. (2020).

Kuo, C.D.L., Teo, E.G. (2015). Emergence of FinTech and the LASIC principles. *Journal of Financial Perspectives., 3*(3), 24-36.

Luo, X., Li, H., Zhang, J., Shim, J.P. (2010). Examining multi-dimensional trust and multi-faceted risk in initial acceptance of emerging technologies: An empirical study of mobile banking services. *Decis. Support Syst., 49*(2), 222-234.
[http://dx.doi.org/10.1016/j.dss.2010.02.008]

Lwin, M., Wirtz, J., Williams, J.D. (2007). Consumer online privacy concerns and responses: a power–responsibility equilibrium perspective. *J. Acad. Mark. Sci., 35*(4), 572-585.
[http://dx.doi.org/10.1007/s11747-006-0003-3]

Philippon, T. (2015). The Fintech Opportunity; National Bureau of Economic Research Working Paper. *Cambridge: National Bureau of Economic Research.* Available from: http://www.nber.org/papers/w22476.

Razzaque, A., Cummings, R.T., Karolak, M., Hamdan, A. (2020). The Propensity to Use FinTech: Input from Bankers in the Kingdom of Bahrain. *Journal of Information & Knowledge Management, 19*(1), 2040025.
[http://dx.doi.org/10.1142/S0219649220400250]

Ryu, H.S., Chang, Y. (2018). What makes users willing or hesitant to use Fintech?: the moderating effect of user type. *Ind. Manage. Data Syst., 118*(3), 541-569.
[http://dx.doi.org/10.1108/IMDS-07-2017-0325]

Ryu, H. S. (2018). Understanding Benefit and Risk Framework of Fintech Adoption: Comparison of Early Adopters and Late Adopters. In *Proceedings of the 51st Hawaii International Conference on System Sciences.* Waikoloa Village, Hawaii. pp. 3864–3873. Available from: https://scholarspace.manoa.hawaii.

Shao, Z., Zhang, L., Li, X. (2019). *Electron. Commerce Res. Appl.,* 33.

Ming-Yen Teoh, W., Choy Chong, S., Lin, B., Wei Chua, J. (2013). Factors affecting consumers' perception of electronic payment: an empirical analysis. *Internet Res., 23*(4), 465-485.
[http://dx.doi.org/10.1108/IntR-09-2012-0199]

Wang, R., Liu, J., Luo, H. (2020). Fintech development and bank risk taking in China. *Eur. J. Finance,* 1-22.
[http://dx.doi.org/10.1080/1351847X.2020.1805782]

Yuwei, Y., Zhihan, L., Bin, H. (2017). Building investor trust in the P2P lending platform with a focus on Chinese P2P lending platforms. Electron. *Commer. Res., 18*(2), 203-224.

Zavolokina, L., Dolata, M., Schwabe, G. (2016). FinTech - What' s in a name? *Thirty Seventh International Conference on Information Systems.*
[http://dx.doi.org/10.5167/uzh-126806]

CHAPTER 4

Transforming Banking with AI Expert Systems Neural Networks and Beyond

Nurideen Alhassan[1,*]

[1] *Accountancy Department, Tamale Technical University, Tamale, Ghana*

Abstract: AI is an advanced technology that has emerged as a groundbreaking innovation. This chapter seeks to examine the impact of AI on the banking sector, specifically focusing on the effects of various dimensions or methods of AI, such as expert systems (ES), neural networks (NN), genetic algorithms (GA), and intelligent agents (IA), on the finance and banking sectors. The AI business has experienced significant growth due to the increased adoption of new technological breakthroughs, leading to its widespread implementation across several domains. The utilisation of artificial intelligence technologies holds the capacity to fundamentally transform the operational framework of the banking industry, thereby augmenting the overall performance of banks. AI is commonly known for its ability to emulate human-like decision-making and minimise errors, which generates considerable enthusiasm among individuals. AI has been adopted to varying degrees across different industries, with the banking industry emerging as one of the notable adopters and implementers of this technology. This literature study provides a comprehensive definition of artificial intelligence (AI), elucidates its current benefits, methods and the influence of AI in the banking sector within the banking sector, and delineates the specific effects it has on banks' overall performance.

Keywords: Artificial intelligence (AI), AI in banking sector, AI technologies, Expert systems (ES), Genetic algorithms, Neural networks.

INTRODUCTION

Technological advancements are being developed at an accelerated rate. The utilisation of AI in the banking sector is comprehensive, encompassing several areas such as the front office, middle office, and back office. The use of AI in the banking and finance sectors has become increasingly prevalent due to advancements in technology. AI applications, such as chatbots, have been implemented to enhance customer service and streamline various banking processes. In the front office, AI is employed in the form of voice assistants and biometrics. In the middle office, AI aids in anti-fraud risk monitoring and facilitates complex legal and compliance workflows. Lastly, in the back office, AI is crucial in credit underwriting through the implementation of smart contract infrastructure. It is projected that banks will achieve cost savings of $447 billion

* **Corresponding author Nurideen Alhassan:** Accountancy Department, Tamale Technical University, Tamale, Ghana; E-mail: aldeen91@hotmail.co.uk

Abdul-Razak Abubakari, Mohammed Majeed, Nurideen Alhassan and Jonas Yomboi (Eds.)

by the year 2023 with the implementation of AI technologies. According to Digalaki (2022), a significant proportion, almost 80%, of banks in the United States demonstrate awareness of the potential advantages associated with artificial intelligence (AI). The advent of AI has given rise to a multitude of both advantageous prospects and complex obstacles (Malali & Gopalakrishnan, 2020). The integration of AI into the banking sector has resulted in enhanced sales processes and the advancement of customer relationship management systems, as highlighted by Tarafdar *et al.* (2019). Historically, the emphasis was placed on automating credit scoring, analytics, and the award process (Mehrotra, 2019). However, over time, these capabilities have expanded to encompass the support of internal systems and procedures as well (Caron, 2019). According to Noreen *et al.* (2023), the implementation of appropriate artificial intelligence techniques in the banking sector has the potential to enhance customer service quality and improve bank performance indicators. Karbassi *et al.* (2022) posited that the service industry plays a crucial role in fostering sustainable economic development. This is primarily due to its lower reliance on conventional resources compared to traditional sectors as well as its receptiveness to the implementation of novel and creative business models. According to Birau *et al.* (2021), the banking system plays a crucial role in achieving a sustainable level of development in the global economy. Throughout the course of history, several technical breakthroughs have been instrumental in enhancing production levels within enterprises. The most recent developments in the realm of business encompass automation, industrial robotics, and artificial intelligence. According to Kaur *et al.* (2020), there has been a notable increase in the utilisation of AI in recent years, leading to significant transformations in various industries' operational practises. One of the sectors under consideration is the banking business. Throughout the years, financial institutions have consistently enhanced their operational strategies through the implementation of Financial Technology (FinTech) solutions. This proactive approach enables banks to establish a unique market position and maintain a competitive edge over their industry rivals. Now, banks are required to adapt to the emerging AI-based FinTech solution. According to Koerselman (2023), there exists the possibility of enhanced operational efficiency across several banking functions. The banking industry has experienced significant impacts from AI across a diverse range of operations. Modifications have been done to several operational aspects, including customer services, credit risk management, asset management, document processing, and fraud detection. The advent of AI has presented the banking industry with a range of novel prospects. Numerous banks within the sector are currently seeing advantageous outcomes from the adoption of this emerging technology (Tiwari & Saxina, 2021). AI has the potential to supplant human labour in certain domains, namely in jobs that need adaptability, contextual understanding, and organisational effectiveness.

These tasks are currently witnessing a gradual shift towards reliance on AI as people increasingly delegate them to artificial intelligence systems. Simultaneously, there has been a transformation of certain tasks within the HR workflow that were not historically recognised as tasks. This transformation enables the utilisation of AI tools for the execution of these duties (Agrawal *et al.*, 2019a, 2019b). Therefore, this study seeks to examine the impact of AI on the banking sector while also elucidating the specific effects of several AI dimensions or methodologies, namely expert systems (ES), neural networks (NN), genetic algorithms (GA), and intelligent agents (IA), on the banking and financial services industry.

The Contribution

The objective of this study is to determine whether the integration of Artificial Intelligence in the banking industry has a favourable influence on both the financial institution and its customers. The favourable impact of AI on the banking industry has raised questions regarding its specific effects on both bankers and customers in relation to their transactions. Chatbots are effectively addressing consumer queries in a prompt manner, providing comprehensive information regarding loans, and highlighting the advancements that have occurred following the integration of AI in banking institutions. Following the integration of AI into the banking sector, several challenges and benefits have emerged for both customers and financial institutions. This inquiry seeks to explore the problems encountered by customers and banks in the wake of AI implementation as well as the factors that have significantly enhanced banking transactions.

Artificial Intelligence

As stated by Tuomi (2018), AI can be defined as a computer system with the ability to understand and interpret auditory signals and verbal inputs. In addition, AI demonstrates problem-solving capabilities, has the aptitude to recognise medical ailments, operates vehicles independently, participates in strategic games like chess, and even reproduces impressionistic artwork influenced by the artistic style of Van Gogh. Intelligent machines, as per their definition, pertain to a system that exhibits the capacity to do tasks that are commonly associated with living organisms. Shi (2019) defines "AI" as the academic discipline concerned with the emulation of fundamental human learning capacities and the investigation of computer responses to specific behaviours. AI pertains to the emulation of human intelligence in computer systems, enabling them to do tasks that traditionally require human cognitive capabilities, such as learning, reasoning, and problem-solving. The domain of information technology has undergone a substantial metamorphosis as a result of advancements in artificial intelligence methodologies. Artificial Intelligence (AI), a specialised branch within the discipline of computer science, involves the advancement of intelligent systems and software that exhibit characteristics and capabilities like those of human beings (Kamble & Shah, 2018). This field of research is usually known as a scientific discipline that aims to develop individuals' abilities in areas such as reasoning, organisation, learning, and perception. AI is designed with the primary objective of augmenting the skills and abilities of human workers rather than displacing them. This is accomplished by developing connections across complex programmes as well as between individuals, computers, comprehension, and the tangible surroundings. One of the primary capabilities of AI lies in its capacity to enable the efficient dissemination and retrieval of data while also providing assistance in diverse activities including data analysis, product development, industrial processes, and scheduling. It is crucial to acknowledge that AI systems depend significantly on human experiences and knowledge in order to discern and choose appropriate logical models. According to Shaw *et al.* (2019), although contemporary AI systems can be perceived as an extension of human interactions, their inability to replicate human emotions prevents them from completely supplanting such interactions. AI is currently attracting considerable attention and creating substantial interest within the banking and finance sectors. Furthermore, in order to provide sound reasoning and support for the argument, the incorporation of artificial intelligence, image recognition, and language processing technologies within the field of AI banking has resulted in substantial changes within the domains of business and employment. Moreover, these technological innovations possess the capacity to provide substantial outcomes for financial institutions, encompassing improvements in operational effectiveness, customer satisfaction, and workforce motivation.

In the finance and banking sectors, artificial intelligence (AI) technologies like expert systems (ES), neural networks (NN), genetic algorithms (GA), and intelligent agents (IA) have gained substantial traction due to their ability to improve decision-making, automate processes, and enhance predictive capabilities. These technologies help in various aspects, from risk management and fraud detection to personalized customer service and algorithmic trading. Below, I'll discuss each of these AI components and their applications in finance and banking.

Expert Systems (ES)

Expert systems are AI applications that emulate the decision-making abilities of a human expert. In finance and banking, they are typically used for credit scoring, fraud detection, loan approvals, and regulatory compliance. For instance, expert systems can analyze a customer's credit history, financial behaviors, and other relevant data to assess their creditworthiness. They can also help identify suspicious activities or unusual transactions that might signal fraud. In the loan approval process, expert systems assist in automating decision-making by evaluating an applicant's risk profile against predefined rules. Additionally, expert systems ensure that financial institutions comply with regulations by analyzing transactions and flagging potentially non-compliant activities. The primary benefit of expert systems in banking is their ability to consistently apply rules and processes without human bias, ensuring fair and efficient decisions.

Neural Networks (NN)

Neural networks, a subset of machine learning, are designed to recognize patterns in large datasets by mimicking the structure of the human brain. In finance and banking, neural networks are used for predictive analytics, risk management, fraud detection, and algorithmic trading. For example, neural networks can forecast stock prices, currency exchange rates, and interest rates by learning from historical data and detecting complex patterns that traditional statistical models might miss. They are also employed to model and predict various types of risks, such as credit risk or market risk. Additionally, neural networks can be trained to detect unusual patterns of transactions that may indicate fraudulent activity. In high-frequency trading, neural networks help make real-time trading decisions based on detected market trends and conditions. The advantage of neural networks lies in their ability to improve performance as they are exposed to more data, making them highly effective in environments with vast amounts of complex data.

Genetic Algorithms (GA)

Genetic algorithms are optimization techniques inspired by the process of natural selection. They are particularly useful in finance and banking for portfolio optimization, option pricing, and market forecasting. In portfolio optimization, genetic algorithms help find the best combination of assets that maximize returns while minimizing risks. In derivative markets, they can be used to solve complex optimization problems related to pricing options or structuring deals. Genetic algorithms are also applied to identify market trends or optimal investment strategies by evolving through different possible scenarios. The strength of genetic algorithms lies in their ability to explore a wide range of possible solutions and find optimal or near-optimal results, even in highly complex problem spaces.

Intelligent Agents (IA)

Intelligent agents are systems that autonomously perform tasks or make decisions based on environmental conditions and objectives. In finance and banking, intelligent agents are applied in various ways, such as customer service, market monitoring, personalized financial advice, and robo-advisory services. AI-powered chatbots and virtual assistants can provide personalized services to customers by answering queries, making recommendations, and assisting with transactions. Intelligent agents can also monitor financial markets for opportunities, reacting to changes in stock prices, news, and market sentiment. Additionally, they analyze individual financial profiles to provide tailored investment recommendations or financial planning services. Robo-advisors, which are automated systems, use algorithms to offer financial advice based on a client's risk tolerance, financial goals, and preferences. The key advantage of intelligent agents is their ability to automate tasks, reduce operational costs, and provide real-time services without requiring direct human oversight.

Combined Impact on the Finance and Banking Sectors

Together, these AI technologies have the potential to revolutionize the finance and banking industries by enhancing decision-making, improving customer experiences, and increasing operational efficiency. AI systems enable faster, more accurate decisions by processing large datasets and uncovering insights that might be overlooked by human analysts. Automation of tasks like loan underwriting, fraud detection, and customer service reduces operational costs for financial institutions. Moreover, AI allows for more personalized services, quicker responses, and better financial advice, ultimately enhancing customer satisfaction. By providing advanced predictive models and real-time data analysis, AI also helps financial institutions assess and manage risks more effectively, thereby preventing losses and fraud. Finally, AI systems play a critical role in ensuring compliance with regulations by continuously monitoring transactions, auditing records, and detecting potential breaches.

Challenges and Considerations

Despite the many benefits, AI adoption in finance and banking also presents several challenges. One major concern is data privacy and security, as the use of large amounts of sensitive financial data raises the risk of privacy breaches and cybersecurity threats. Additionally, AI models, particularly those based on historical data, may inherit biases, leading to unfair or discriminatory outcomes. Regulatory uncertainty is another issue, as the legal and ethical frameworks surrounding AI in finance are still evolving, making it difficult for institutions to ensure compliance. Financial organizations must navigate these challenges carefully to ensure the responsible and ethical use of AI technologies.

The Impact of Artificial Intelligence on Finance and Banking

In recent times, there has been a notable emergence of technical progress that has paved the way for the integration of AI in facilitating corporate cognitive computing. This entails the incorporation of programmes into apps with the purpose of aiding and enhancing organisational operations (Tarafdar *et al.*, 2019). This encompasses enhancing the efficiency of information analysis, acquiring data outputs that are more precise and dependable, and enabling employees to engage in jobs of a higher degree. In recent years, the efficacy and practicality of AI-based technology have been demonstrated. Nevertheless, a significant number of business executives continue to exhibit a deficiency in understanding the strategic use of AI within their respective organisations. According to Gulen (2023), AI is playing a transformative role in the banking sector, propelling it into a new era characterised by digitization. The implementation of this technology has the capacity to enhance the efficiency, security, and personalization of banking operations. This blog post aims to examine the effects of AI solutions within the banking industry, emphasising the advantages, implementations, obstacles, and potential advancements (Jenner, 2018). The influence of artificial intelligence in the banking industry has been profound, resulting in a variety of advantages such as greater customer experiences, improved operational efficiency, and heightened security measures. The banking industry has experienced a notable influence from artificial intelligence, mostly in the form of enhanced client experiences that are both personalised and convenient (Gulen, 2023). Financial institutions can enhance customer satisfaction by leveraging AI-powered chatbots and virtual assistants, which enable them to offer round-th--clock client care and minimise waiting periods. Artificial intelligence algorithms have the capacity to furnish personalised financial guidance, and tailor-made product suggestions, and even forecast consumers' financial requirements, empowering financial institutions to deliver customised offerings and services (Tang & Tien, 2020). The financial services sector has undergone substantial transformations in order to align with the evolving demands and preferences of customers. Historically, the provision of services to clients was confined to conventional products and services. However, in the present era of digitalization, customers have developed higher expectations, seeking more inventive and contextually appropriate services. The adoption of digital transformation in traditional banks has become increasingly prevalent with the integration of AI technologies. This implementation allows banks to acquire valuable insights about their clients, including their wants and preferences. Consequently, banks are able to enhance their services and improve their capacity to attract new customers

(Kumar, 2018). Banks employ AI techniques to customise their products and advertisements in accordance with client demand and behaviour. This is achieved by integrating data from several sources, including transaction history, previous inquiries, geographical location, search history, and even social media platforms. AI effectively caters to customers' banking needs by comprehending their specific requirements (Tang & Tien, 2020). Artificial intelligence has the capability to analyse many forms of data, enabling it to derive valuable insights pertaining to client behaviours and interests. Historical data is of utmost importance in identifying the purchasing behaviours of consumers that are necessary for delivering the anticipated bank products and services. Traditional banks mostly maintain their primary transactional relationships with consumers through the provision of deposit and payment services. According to Kumar (2018), AI has contributed to increased efficiency within the banking sector by facilitating the automation of repetitive operations and processes. This encompasses several responsibilities such as data entry, fraud detection, and compliance monitoring, allowing staff to allocate their efforts towards more intricate assignments. According to Gulen (2023), AI-powered systems possess the capability to analyse extensive volumes of data in real time, thereby facilitating financial institutions' identification of patterns and trends that would otherwise be unattainable by manual means. This can aid institutions in making more informed judgments and enhancing their risk management practices. Financial institutions are currently investigating the utilisation of AI in order to visually represent data derived from legal papers or annual reports. Additionally, they are studying AI's potential to extract significant clauses from these documents. AI technologies independently generate models by observing data and conducting backtesting in order to learn from past errors and enhance their accuracy.

Benefits of AI in the Banking and Financial Services Sector

Enhanced Operational Effectiveness and Financial Benefits

Enhanced operational effectiveness and financial benefits are achieved by implementing automated processes and optimisation techniques. AI has the capability to automate repetitive operations, such as the input and analysis of data, allowing personnel to allocate their efforts towards more intricate and demanding assignments. This not only enhances operational efficiency and cost-effectiveness but also mitigates the likelihood of errors and enhances the precision of data processing.

Improved Assessment of Investments

Interest revenue is just one aspect of the broader spectrum of income production. Consequently, financial institutions are consistently seeking profitable investment prospects in order to generate a favourable rate of return. The appropriate investing software has the capability to offer investment suggestions that align with the risk tolerance of these institutions. Furthermore, the ability to effectively assess client funding requests is crucial, particularly considering the inherent complexity of industry-specific data. The responsibility for making investment decisions remains with human experts. Investment analysis software facilitates the procedure and allows for the inclusion of a greater number of factors. When an institution has interests beyond its national boundaries, the process of acquiring information can become time-consuming. Evaluating a novel environment can present difficulties; however, the utilisation of appropriate AI software plays a crucial role in expediting this undertaking.

Enhancing the Process of Decision-Making

AI algorithms provide the capability to effectively examine vast quantities of data, thereby offering significant insights to financial organisations. These insights encompass customer behaviour patterns, market trends, and risk assessments (Gulen, 2023). This facilitates the ability of institutions to enhance decision-making processes and formulate more efficient strategies in order to effectively address the evolving demands of clients and the industry. Enhanced decision-making is facilitated by the utilisation of data analysis and insights.

Efficient Fraud Detection

AI is again responsible for the identification and prevention of fraudulent activities. It is not unexpected that AI has superior capabilities in managing extensive datasets and identifying instances of fraud well in advance of its human counterparts. According to Stanra Tech Solutions Pvt. Ltd. (2023), several algorithms can be proficiently employed to execute repetitive activities without errors. Banking and financial institutions are currently reaping the advantages of being a data-intensive industry. Banking-related fraud is a significant threat to both the general public and the banking industry. The recovery process for individuals impacted by financial fraud is often arduous due to the substantial challenges involved in recovering from monetary losses. In the event of detecting any fraudulent transaction inside a bank statement, it is incumbent upon us to expeditiously notify the bank. The banking authorities implemented stringent measures to address the issue. The establishment of trust between a consumer and their bank fosters a sense of reliability, thereby cultivating a long-term relationship between the two parties. The utilisation of Artificial Intelligence in the financial sector enables the realisation of these possibilities. The increasing utility of this system is evidenced by its ability to enable banks to effectively identify instances of fraud and thereafter implement appropriate measures to address them.

Good Customer Experience

The concept of "customer experience" refers to the overall perception and impression that customers have of a company or brand based on their interactions and encounters. It has enhanced client satisfaction through the implementation of personalised and automated processes. Artificial intelligence (AI)-enabled chatbots and virtual assistants have the capability to deliver customised and automated services to clients. These services encompass addressing inquiries, offering financial guidance, and facilitating transactions. According to Gulen (2023), the provision ofprompt, effective, and customised services that are accessible round the clock contributes to the improvement of the customer experience.

Security

The implementation of robust fraud detection and prevention measures has led to a significant improvement in security. The banking industry accumulates a substantial volume of data, necessitating the implementation of robust security measures to prevent any breaches or infringements. It is crucial to choose a suitable technology partner that possesses a comprehensive understanding of both AI and the banking industry. Additionally, it is essential to consider a partner that provides a diverse range of security measures to effectively safeguard customer data and ensure its proper handling. AI algorithms provide the capability to analyse substantial volumes of client data in real time for the purpose of detecting potential instances of fraudulent conduct, such as atypical spending behaviours or transactions that arouse suspicion. The implementation of this measure aids financial institutions in proactively mitigating fraudulent activities, thereby bolstering security measures and safeguarding the interests of both clients and the institution.

The Automation of Investment Processes

Several prominent organisations, such as UBS and ING, have ventured into a potentially hazardous and unexplored industry in order to explore novel prospects. These firms have successfully created AI systems that effectively automate investment processes. According to Stanra Tech Solutions Pvt Ltd. (2023), this technology is continuously monitored by human operators and facilitates the discovery of novel prospects through enhanced modelling techniques.

Risk Management and Compliance

AI has the potential to be employed in the banking sector for the purpose of risk management and compliance. AI algorithms possess the capability to effectively analyse vast quantities of data, enabling them to detect and discern possible dangers, such as credit defaults or market swings (Gulen, 2023). This facilitates the decision-making process for institutions and enhances the development of more efficient risk management techniques. AI has the ability to assist institutions in meeting regulatory obligations through the automation of compliance procedures and the detection of potential infractions of compliance standards.

Monitoring and Analysing Market Trends

The integration of artificial intelligence and machine learning technologies in the financial services sector enables banks to efficiently handle substantial amounts of data and make accurate predictions regarding current market trends. Sophisticated machine learning methodologies facilitate the assessment of market sentiments and provide recommendations for investment opportunities. AI solutions in the banking sector provide recommendations on optimal stock investment timing and issue alerts regarding potential risks. The developing technology discussed herein possesses a notable data processing capacity, facilitating expedited decision-making processes and enhancing the convenience of trading activities for both financial institutions and their clientele.

Automated Customer Service

The concept of "automated customer service" refers to the utilisation of technology and computer systems to provide assistance and support to customers in a self-service manner. The availability of a 24/7 chatbot eliminates the concern of consumers over the necessity to contact the bank within limited operating hours, including closing time, holidays, and weekends. Additionally, it implies that the extensively documented chatbot possesses a greater capacity to effectively resolve consumer issues compared to a live customer care representative (Stanra Tech Solutions Pvt Ltd., 2023). Although chatbots have been in existence for some time, their integration within financial institutions provides them with a distinct advantage in managing various routine banking operations that were previously reliant on human intervention.

Tailored Banking Experiences

AI has the potential to offer customers tailored banking experiences. According to Gulen (2023), the utilisation of artificial intelligence algorithms enables the provision of personalised financial advice and product recommendations through the analysis of consumer data. This approach improves the overall satisfaction of customers by offering customised services that cater to their specific needs and preferences.

Enhanced Adherence to Regulatory Standards

Governments employ their regulatory authority to ensure that banks are effectively mitigating large-scale defaults and preventing consumers from engaging in any form of financial misconduct. Banks adhere to specific restrictions in order to prevent illicit activities, and AI has played a significant role in facilitating this process (Stanra Tech Solutions Pvt Ltd, 2023). Financial institutions leverage smart AI virtual assistants to effectively monitor transactions, ensuring compliance with regulatory requirements while also monitoring client habits. This enables individuals to engage in compliant behaviour while simultaneously reducing the total level of risk involved.

Loan Underwriting and Credit Analysis

The process of loan underwriting and credit analysis involves the evaluation and assessment of a borrower's creditworthiness and the associated risks of granting a loan. AI has the potential to be employed for loan underwriting and credit research within the banking sector. According to Gulen (2023), the utilisation of AI algorithms enables the examination of client data to evaluate credit risk and ascertain the probability of loan default. This facilitates financial firms' enhancement of decision-making processes and the formulation of more efficient credit analysis procedures.

Customer Satisfaction

The concept of customer satisfaction refers to the degree to which customers perceive their needs and expectations to be fulfilled by a product or service. Ensuring customer happiness is a fundamental and crucial objective for banks worldwide. In the event that customers express dissatisfaction with banking services, banks may incur significant financial losses. The long-term operation and effectiveness of a bank are contingent upon customer satisfaction. Ensuring customer happiness is of utmost importance to every financial institution. Banks offer high-quality and customised services to each individual consumer. In contemporary times, Artificial Intelligence assumes a crucial and irreplaceable function in this context. Firms have the potential to enhance their revenue through the utilisation of this resource. Additionally, it is beneficial to establish and sustain a positive client relationship as well as manage a well-structured and efficient back office.

The Reduction of Operational Costs

Although the banking business primarily operates in a digital manner, certain tasks necessitate human intervention as they cannot be automated. Banks may encounter significant operational expenses and vulnerabilities stemming from human fallibility. According to Stanra Tech Solutions Pvt. Ltd. (2023), automation is not feasible for certain operations. However, rule-based digital tasks that necessitate human participation can be combined with other artificial intelligence techniques to enhance outcomes. For instance, operations that include a significant amount of paperwork possess the capacity to be automated when natural language processing achieves the capability to effectively interpret handwriting and execute processes using a rule-based approach.

AI Methods/Dimensions Used in Finance and Banking

Speech Recognition

This feature, sometimes referred to as automatic speech recognition (ASR), computer speech recognition, or voice-to-text, utilises natural language processing (NLP) to convert spoken language into written language (IBM, 2021). Numerous mobile devices integrate speech recognition technology into their operating systems in order to facilitate voice search functionality and enhance accessibility in text-based communication. According to Chowdhury (2023), the utilisation of machine learning and natural language processing algorithms enables the comprehension of client preferences, the anticipation of their requirements, and the provision of tailored recommendations.

The Genetic Algorithm (GA)

An algorithm refers to a prescribed collection of instructions that are iteratively executed in order to solve a given problem. The term "genetic" pertains to the behaviour shown by algorithms that bear resemblance to biological processes. Furthermore, this approach draws inspiration from Darwin's idea of natural selection in order to address optimisation challenges, particularly those characterised by incomplete or limited knowledge, as well as constrained computational capabilities (Kumar, 2018). According to O'Brien (2000), Genetic Algorithms (GAs) can be described as problem-solving techniques that facilitate the generation of solutions to specific issues by employing procedures that are compatible with the given context. Ajam (2018) asserts that genetic algorithms (GAs) are designed to mimic human problem-solving processes through the manipulation and reorganisation of component parts. This is achieved by employing techniques such as reproduction, transformation, and natural selection. Consequently, GAs offer a means to explore all potential combinations of numbers in order to identify the most suitable non-numeric variables that represent an optimal problem structure. These algorithms prove particularly valuable. Financial institutions, particularly hedge funds and proprietary traders, have employed algorithmic trading, also known as black-box trading, for the purpose of conducting trades. The utilisation of mathematical models for the purpose of automated response to dynamic market situations, wherein positions are opened and closed based on predetermined parameters without human intervention, has been described by Tang and Tien (2020). Algorithmic trading has been extensively utilised by major financial organisations, including investment banks and investment funds, to enhance efficiency and achieve optimal pricing. This practise offers significant advantages to both the company and its consumers by facilitating speedier execution of trades at the most favourable prices. The benefits associated with these transactions include enhanced precision and reduced errors, automated assessment of numerous market situations concurrently, and a decrease in errors stemming from psychological or emotional factors. The predominant use of artificial intelligence (AI) lies within the realm of data analytics, where algorithms are employed to find and evaluate patterns, facilitating the acquisition of business-relevant insights. By utilising data analytics, corporations have the capability to forecast the potential purchases of customers, detect instances of credit fraud in real time, and automate the customization of digital advertisements. Tasks of this nature frequently exceed the capabilities of human beings, hence lacking the potential to present a substantial jeopardy to employment opportunities for humans (Davenport & Ronanki, 2018).

Recommendation Engines

Recommendation engines, often known as recommender systems, are computational tools that provide personalised suggestions to users based on their preferences. By using historical consumption patterns, artificial intelligence algorithms have the potential to identify data trends that can be utilised in the formulation of enhanced cross-selling tactics (IBM, 2021). The purpose of this tool is to provide pertinent supplementary suggestions to customers at the time of checkout in the context of e-commerce platforms.

The AI System for Recommendation

The exponential expansion of information available on the World Wide Web, along with the swift proliferation of e-services, has presented users with an extensive array of options, necessitating more intricate decision-making processes. Recommender systems are primarily designed to aid those lacking experience or knowledge in navigating the extensive range of choices they encounter (Lu *et al.*, 2015). Recommender systems utilise several sources of information in order to make predictions about users' preferences for things of interest (Shapira *et al.*, 2011). The initial application of recommender systems was in the field of e-commerce, with the aim of addressing the issue of information overload resulting from the emergence of Web 2.0. Subsequently, its utilisation was swiftly extended to encompass the personalization of many domains such as e-government, e-business, e-learning, and e-tourism (Lu *et al.*, 2015). In contemporary times, recommender systems have become an essential component of various online platforms, including but not limited to Amazon.com, YouTube, Netflix, Yahoo, Facebook, Last.fm, and Meetup. Recommender systems are specifically engineered to assess the value of an item and make predictions on its suitability for recommendation (Adomavicius & Tuzhilin, 2005; Chowdhury, 2022).

Conversational Agent

A conversational agent, commonly referred to as a "chatbot," is an automated computer programme. Chatbots are computer programmes that have the capability to engage in written or verbal communication with human users through natural language (Shawar & Atwell, 2007). In the event of a matter or inquiry pertaining to the products or services offered by banking institutions, consumers are required to engage with the designated officers in order to seek a resolution for the issue at hand. Nevertheless, this procedure might be characterised as laborious, monotonous, and time-consuming. The chatbot is constructed using a natural language processing system and utilises a chatlog. These assistants possess the ability to comprehend the specific vocabulary used in the context of financial services, as well as interpret customer demands pertaining to monetary matters. Over the course of time, a group of proficient individuals specialising in algorithms, platforms, and customer service have developed an extensive and intricate collection of chatbots with the aim of improving chatbot performance (Tang & Tien, 2020). The utilisation of AI-driven chatbots and virtual assistants is experiencing a notable surge in popularity within the banking sector (Noreen *et al.*, 2023). Organisations have the capability to offer clients individualised and automated services, encompassing tasks such as responding to inquiries, delivering financial guidance, and facilitating transactions. According to Gulen (2023), chatbots have the capability to be seamlessly incorporated into messaging applications or websites, thereby offering prompt and effective services that are accessible at all times. This not only improves the overall satisfaction of customers but also alleviates the burden on human personnel, enabling them to allocate their efforts towards more intricate responsibilities. The utilisation of chatbots in the banking industry offers numerous advantages, primarily centred around enhancing customer relationships, fostering the development of mobile banking services, and promoting additional utilities. It also improves consumer experience by incorporating interactive elements, such as human interaction. In order to enhance the effectiveness of customer interactions, banks can accumulate customer knowledge by developing a repository of questions that the chatbot can utilise. This will enable the chatbot to provide more sophisticated responses, thereby improving its overall performance (Tang & Tien, 2020). By doing so, banks can simultaneously reduce costs and enhance customer service levels, which is particularly crucial given the growing number of customers and businesses. The enhancement of job satisfaction can be achieved by allocating customer service personnel to higher-value jobs. The application of AI-based banking technology has resulted in significant breakthroughs across several industries, yielding positive outcomes for enterprises. Additionally, Watson, a creation of IBM, has been specifically engineered to respond to user inquiries. This is accomplished through the use of machine learning techniques and natural language processing (NLP), which facilitate the retrieval of information and the representation of inherent domain knowledge. The implementation of these automated bots is advantageous in enhancing customer service and has already been adopted by a majority of prominent and expanding financial institutions (Singh *et al.*, 2018).

Intelligent Automation

The concept of "intelligent automation" refers to the integration of artificial intelligence and automation technologies to enhance operational efficiency and decision-making processes. The term "intelligent automation" refers to software that possesses the capability to make decisions inside a designated business unit in a manner that is equivalent to human decision-making. As an illustration, an intelligent manufacturing robot would not merely repeat its human tasks but rather perform them based on real-time data and independently manage faults and exceptions (Javed, 2015).

Automated Stock Trading

The concept of automated stock trading refers to the use of computer algorithms and software programmes to execute buy and sell orders in financial markets. The utilisation of artificial intelligence (AI) in the domain of stock trading is a well-established practice that has been in existence for a considerable period of time. In the past, only economically stable and huge corporations had the means to procure it. The primary goal of engaging in stock market trading is to generate financial gains. Emotional elements are not taken into consideration throughout the decision-making process of purchasing and/or selling stocks. According to Chowdhury (2021), the inclusion of emotions such as greed and fear in the decision-making process by individuals often leads to erroneous decisions, resulting in negative consequences (Lieder, 2018). AI-driven high-frequency trading systems have been developed with the primary objective of maximising the efficiency of stock portfolios. These platforms operate autonomously, executing a significant number of deals on a daily basis, ranging from hundreds to even millions, without any human involvement (IBM, 2021). Through the utilisation of artificial intelligence (AI) algorithms and machine learning methodologies, traders are empowered to efficiently and precisely analyse extensive volumes of data, resulting in enhanced decision-making capabilities about investment opportunities (Lieder, 2018). The aforementioned developments have led to enhanced operational effectiveness, diminished expenses associated with transactions, and heightened financial gains inside the stock market. The capacity of artificial intelligence (AI) to process vast amounts of data in real time is a significant benefit in the context of stock trading (Chowdhury, 2021). Artificial intelligence algorithms possess the ability to monitor a multitude of data sources, encompassing financial accounts, news reports, social media sentiments, and market movements, with the purpose of discerning patterns and extracting valuable information. This enables traders to promptly respond to market movements, such as variations in stock prices or unforeseen occurrences, and adapt their investing strategy accordingly (Lieder, 2018). By utilising artificial intelligence (AI), investors have the ability to maintain a competitive advantage and enhance their trading decisions through increased access to information. In addition, trading systems driven by artificial intelligence are specifically engineered to acquire knowledge and adjust their strategies based on past data, facilitating a constant enhancement of their ability to make informed decisions.

Neural Network (NN)

The field of finance exhibits a significant degree of nonlinearity, and at times, the observed information concerning stock prices may appear to be entirely stochastic in nature. In their study, Hawley *et al.* (1990) utilised neural networks (NNs) to provide a novel approach to assist economic decision-makers operating in dynamic contexts, namely within the transport and shipping sectors. There is a clear necessity for collaborative endeavours between the financial sector and neural networks (NNs). The latest iterations may demonstrate attributes that, to some extent, emulate the behaviour of the actual world. The real world is explained by psychophysical features that are also derived from individual human beings (Lieder, 2018). According to Palaniappan (2018), conventional time series techniques like ARIMA and GARCH models are only viable under the assumption of stationarity. This assumption necessitates preprocessing the series by applying transformations such as taking log returns. Nevertheless, a significant challenge comes when attempting to include these models in a real-time trading system, as the presence of non-stationarity cannot be guaranteed with the continuous addition of fresh data. The issue can be addressed through the utilisation of neural networks, as they possess the capability to operate without necessitating stationarity. Moreover, neural networks possess inherent efficacy in discerning the interconnections among data and using this ability to make predictions or classify novel data.

Augmented Reality

Augmented reality (AR) refers to a technology that superimposes computer-generated sensory information, such as visuals and sounds. Numerous sectors have begun incorporating cutting-edge technology to augment their commercial endeavours, bestowing a remarkable advantage on their business operations. Augmented reality (AR) is a technology that enhances human vision and facilitates communication by providing virtual assistance. It offers a means to alleviate complex real-world problems by revealing additional facts. Augmented reality has been implemented across various industries, including healthcare, games, and media, with the aim of enhancing and streamlining current procedures. This application can be implemented for business development in industries characterised by high-cost operations and high-risk engagement (Heng, 2015). Banking and finance institutions utilise augmented reality technology to gain insights into client performance and effectively present recommendations aimed at improving consumers' spending habits (Dubey, 2019).

Computer Vision

Computer vision is a field of study that focuses on enabling computers to interpret and understand visual information from digital images or videos. Ajam (2018) asserts that computer vision pertains to the facilitation of information acquisition by machines using visual means, involving the analysis of images or videos to enable prediction and pattern recognition (Nilsson, 2009). It is imperative to differentiate the notion under discussion from image processing, as the latter primarily focuses on generating an image based on an existing one, whereas computer vision is concerned with comprehending the underlying events or phenomena (Machine Learning Mastery, 2019). This AI technology facilitates the extraction of significant information from digital photos, movies, and other visual inputs, enabling computers and systems to subsequently initiate actions based on these inputs. The capability to offer suggestions sets it apart from activities related to picture recognition (IBM, 2021). Computer vision, which utilises convolutional neural networks, finds its utility in various domains such as social media for photo tagging, healthcare for radiological imaging, and the automotive sector for self-driving cars. Computer vision encompasses a range of tasks and domains, including but not limited to character recognition for automated licence plate reading in the context of traffic violations, machine inspection for assessing the readiness of aircraft exteriors prior to flight, retail applications such as product recognition for seamless automated checkout systems like those employed in Amazon Go stores, warehouse logistics for the development of autonomous package delivery systems, medical imaging.

Intelligent Agents

Intelligent agents, often known as artificial intelligence (AI) agents, are entities that possess the ability to observe their surrounding environment through the utilisation of sensors. Subsequently, these agents are capable of responding to their surroundings by employing actuators or prey mechanisms. The concept being discussed is a knowledge-based expert system that is integrated into computer-based information systems to enhance intelligence. Additionally, it may be described as a programme or methodology designed for end-users to facilitate the execution of various tasks (Petropoulos, 2018). Artificial intelligence (AI) refers to the repository of information pertaining to a particular individual or process that is used to make informed judgements and successfully execute tasks in order to fulfil the objectives of the user. Artificial Intelligence (AI) can be defined as a system that utilises sensors and actuators to perceive and interact with its surroundings, hence exhibiting a programmed behaviour. Shaw *et al.* (2019) emphasise the role of software applications in facilitating the execution of Internet-based transactions within a corporation. These apps serve to monitor and manage buying and selling activities, while also providing users with timely alerts regarding significant events (Aljaber, 2020). Currently, a plethora of artificial intelligence (AI) applications can be observed within operating systems, including various domains such as software applications, email systems, and cell phone programmes.

The Future of AI in Banking and Finance

The prospective trajectory of Artificial Intelligence (AI) within the domains of finance and banking.

Banks are compelled to promptly embark on their artificial intelligence endeavours, given the imperative to remain competitive in a future characterised by a proliferation of cutting-edge and inventive technologies. The application of artificial intelligence in the financial sector is still in its nascent phase, with ample opportunities for expansion and advancement. The following are prospective advancements in the application of artificial intelligence within the banking sector: There have been several advancements observed in the methods of communication, customer assistance, recruitment, and asset management within the financial sector. In contemporary times, stock investment and finance are predominantly characterised by the significance of technical expertise and fortuitous outcomes. In the future, advancements in sentiment analysis, crowd-sourced data, and algorithms are expected to revolutionise the way financial transactions are conducted. The impact of the AI revolution extends beyond the financial sector and banking business, encompassing a diverse range of sectors. Several notable advancements in the business encompass the use of automated anaesthesia distribution for routine procedures, which not only aids in cost reduction but also enhances patient care. Additionally, the introduction of self-driving vehicles has been facilitated by digital guidance systems. These advancements would enable organisations to automate mundane and laborious tasks, such as completing forms and conducting back-end testing.

The use of voice assistants, exemplified by Amazon's Alexa and Google Home, is experiencing a notable surge in adoption inside residential settings. There is potential for the integration of AI-powered voice assistants with financial services in the future, which might enhance the convenience and efficiency of the banking experience for customers. The emergence of financial technology (fintech) firms has caused significant disruption within the conventional banking sector, with a notable trend of these startups leveraging artificial intelligence (AI) to create novel offerings and solutions. In forthcoming times, it is plausible that there will be an increase in partnerships between financial institutions and fintech companies, leading to the emergence of novel and inventive applications of artificial intelligence inside the banking sector.

With the ongoing advancements in AI technology, there has been a corresponding enhancement in its capacity to identify and mitigate instances of fraudulent activities. Sophisticated fraud detection algorithms possess the potential to discern and avert novel forms of fraudulent activity that were imperceptible. With the increasing sophistication of AI algorithms, there is potential for enhanced personalization in the realm of banking experiences. This may encompass individualised investment guidance, personalised financial strategizing, and customised product suggestions.

Implications

This study intends to examine the impact of artificial intelligence (AI) in the banking sector and provide a comprehensive understanding of the effects of various dimensions or methods of AI (expert systems, neural networks, genetic algorithms, and intelligent agents) on the banking and financial services industry. Artificial intelligence (AI) possesses significant revolutionary capabilities and presents major implications for global society and the economy. Artificial intelligence (AI) is assuming a progressively significant function in influencing economic and financial sector advancements and is being recognised as a catalyst for productivity and economic expansion by enhancing efficiency, refining decision-making procedures, and fostering the emergence of novel products and businesses. It is advisable for customers to contemplate transitioning to digital transactions due to the prevailing shifts in trends, as it is imperative to remain up-to-date and align with them. In addition, it is imperative for customers to conduct thorough research and stay updated on emerging developments in order to safeguard themselves from potential fraudulent activities. Simultaneously with the implementation of AI in the banking sector, it is imperative for banks to disseminate information and raise awareness among the public regarding this technological advancement. Due to these circumstances, individuals are increasingly utilising this technology, including those who are resistant to change, lack knowledge about its usage, or are apprehensive about its implementation. Consequently, they will become aware of the integration of artificial intelligence (AI) in banking, which aids in the expansion of AI utilisation within the banking industry. Furthermore, this factor contributes to the successful deployment of artificial intelligence in the banking sector. The integration of artificial intelligence (AI) technology in the banking sector incurs significant costs, particularly for private banks, posing challenges to its adoption. In order to foster economic development, it is imperative for the government to allocate funds towards the integration of artificial intelligence (AI) inside the banking sector. This private financial institution places a higher level of significance on the integration of artificial intelligence inside the banking sector. Artificial intelligence (AI) is exerting a profound impact on the financial industry, leading to significant transformations in the realms of financial intermediation, risk management, compliance, and regulatory oversight. In contemporary times, artificial intelligence (AI) has been integrated into banking systems, proving advantageous for customers and increasing awareness among the general populace. The adoption of artificial intelligence (AI) in banks has proven beneficial to customers by facilitating their transactions. Moreover, it has had a favourable influence on banks by streamlining the complexity associated with banking operations. According to the study findings, it is evident that artificial intelligence (AI) facilitates convenient access and streamlines banking transactions. The accessibility of AI technology allows individuals to readily obtain information pertaining to its usage using search engines. Automated transactions have been found to be more effective in minimising errors when compared to manual transactions. The provided information offers a concise and unambiguous description of transactions pertaining to the field of banking. In conclusion, amidst the era of artificial intelligence, it is imperative for both enterprises and individuals to adopt and exploit this technology, recognising its immense capabilities. Organisations that do not successfully adjust their strategies and operations may face negative consequences as a result of disruptive forces. It is imperative for governments and politicians to actively participate in the establishment of regulatory frameworks that effectively tackle ethical concerns, safeguard data privacy, and promote the responsible deployment of artificial intelligence. The influence of artificial intelligence (AI) on several sectors is extensive and significant. The phenomenon is revolutionising our work practices, reshaping the commercial environment, and fundamentally reconfiguring our interaction with technological advancements. The ability to embrace and comprehend the potential of this disruption will be crucial for organisations to maintain competitiveness and flourish in the future, which is characterised by the integration of artificial intelligence.

CONCLUSION

This chapter seeks to examine the impact of artificial intelligence (AI) on the banking sector, specifically focusing on the effects of various dimensions or methods of AI, such as neural networks (NN), genetic algorithms (GA), and intelligent agents (IA), on the banking and financial services industry. In this context, artificial intelligence (AI) is defined as the utilisation of computers to execute tasks that often necessitate human intelligence, encompassing but not limited to learning, reasoning, and problem-solving. The utilisation of artificial intelligence (AI) in the banking sector has experienced a significant expansion in recent years. This trend is driven by financial institutions' pursuit of maintaining competitiveness and adapting to the expanding digital environment in order to cater to the dynamic requirements of their consumers. The banking business is currently undergoing rapid transformation, driven by advancements in artificial intelligence (AI), which are playing a pivotal role in revolutionising the sector. AI technologies have been implemented in the banking sector across various domains, including core banking, operational performance, customer service, and analytics. In the realm of artificial intelligence (AI), the concept of banking has transcended its traditional confines of physical branches, giving rise to a novel landscape of contemporary financial institutions. The use of novel banking services by contemporary financial institutions is facilitating their growth and expansion. The utilisation of technology is facilitating the wider adoption of the financial system, enhancing cost efficiency, and enabling the execution of small-scale transactions. The utilisation of technology in a proficient manner has a magnifying impact on the expansion and advancement of financial institutions. Therefore, the implementation of artificial intelligence has resulted in increased client attraction and facilitated the growth of banks. Banks have the potential to utilise artificial intelligence (AI) in order to enhance the overall client experience by facilitating seamless and continuous client engagement. It is important to note that the application of AI in the banking sector extends beyond just retail banking services. Artificial intelligence (AI) is increasingly being utilised in the back- and middle-office operations of investment banking and other financial supervisory activities. In summary, the incorporation of artificial intelligence within the banking sector presents a multitude of advantages, encompassing heightened consumer satisfaction, bolstered security measures, and amplified operational efficacy. Nevertheless, it is imperative to acknowledge and tackle the obstacles and apprehensions associated with AI in order to guarantee its conscientious and ethical utilisation. The future prospects of artificial intelligence in the banking business appear to be quite favourable, as it has the possibility for many advancements such as enhanced fraud detection capabilities, heightened levels of personalization, integration with voice assistants, and collaborations with fintech firms. As the progression of AI technology persists, it is imperative for financial institutions to remain abreast of the most recent advancements and conscientiously incorporate AI in a manner that is both responsible and ethical.

REFERENCES

Adomavicius, G., Tuzhilin, A. (2005). Toward the next generation of recommender systems: a survey of the state-of-the-art and possible extensions. *IEEE Trans. Knowl. Data Eng.,* *17*(6), 734-749.
[http://dx.doi.org/10.1109/TKDE.2005.99]

Agrawal, A., Gans, J., & Goldfarb, A. (Eds.). (2019a). The economics of artificial intelligence: an agenda. University of Chicago Press.
[http://dx.doi.org/10.7208/chicago/9780226613475.001.0001]

Agrawal, A., Gans, J.S., Goldfarb, A. (2019). Artificial intelligence: the ambiguous labor market impact of automating prediction. *J. Econ. Perspect.,* *33*(2), 31-50. b
[http://dx.doi.org/10.1257/jep.33.2.31]

Ajam, M.D.I.M.H. (2018). Artificial Intelligence and its Implications for High Performance Organizations-Exploratory Study in the Ministry of Science and Technology. *Journal of Administration and Economics,* 115.

Tiwari, A.K., Saxena, D. (2021). Application of Artificial Intelligence in Indian Banks. *International Conference on Computational Performance Evaluation,* 545-548.
[http://dx.doi.org/10.1109/ComPE53109.2021.9751981]

Bobadilla, J., Ortega, F., Hernando, A., Gutiérrez, A. (2013). Recommender systems survey. *Knowl. Base. Syst.,* *46*, 109-132.
[http://dx.doi.org/10.1016/j.knosys.2013.03.012]

Birau, R., Spulbar, C., Karbassi Yazdi, A. (2021). Critical success factors for CRM implementation in the Iranian banking sector: A conceptual analysis, Revista de Științe Politice. *Revue des Sciences Politiques,* *69*, 32-45.

Chowdhury, E. K. (2021). Prospects and challenges of using artificial intelligence in the audit process. In Abedin, M.Z., Hassan, M.K., Hajek, P. (eds.). *The Essentials of Machine Learning in Finance and Accounting*, Routledge. pp. 139-155. Available from: https://tinyurl.com/4stz7ycj.
[http://dx.doi.org/10.4324/9781003037903-8]

Caron, M.S. (2019). The transformative efect of AI on the banking industry. *Banking & Finance Law Review,* *34*(2), 169-214.

Chowdhury, E.K. (2022). Disastrous consequence of coronavirus pandemic on the earning capacity of individuals: an emerging economy perspective. *SN Bus. Econ.,* *2*(10), 153.

[http://dx.doi.org/10.1007/s43546-022-00333-z] [PMID: 36158254]

Dubey, V. (2019). FinTech Innovations in Digital Banking. *Int. J. Eng. Res. Technol. (Ahmedabad), 8*(10), 597-601. [IJERT].

Digalaki, E. (2022). The impact of artifcial intelligence in the banking sector & how AI is being used in 2022. Available from: sider.com/ai-in-banking-report?r=US&IR=T.

Gulen, K. (2023). AI-driven innovation in banking and future opportunities. Available from: https://dataconomy.com/2023/02/15/artificial-intelligence-in-banking-industry/.

Heng, S. (2015). Augmented reality: Specialized applications are the key to this fast-growing market for Germany. Deutsche Bank Research. *Current Issues Sector Research*, 1-14.

Hawley, D.D., Johnson, J.D., Raina, D. (1990). Artificial neural systems: A new tool for financial decision-making. *Financ. Anal. J., 46*(6), 63-72.
[http://dx.doi.org/10.2469/faj.v46.n6.63]

IBM. (2021). Artificial intelligence (AI). Available from: https://www.ibm.com/cloud/learn/what-is-artifici-l-intelligence.

Javed, S. (2015). Intelligent Automation: What it is. Why it matters. Available from: http://www.cio.com/article/2952121/business-processmanagement/intelligent-automation-what-it-is-why-it-m atters.html.

Jenner, G. (2017). AI-enabled world will change reality: airlines underestimating the likely future role of artificial intelligence in day-to-day operations might not only lose out on cost savings and other efficiencies, but also revenue opportunities. *Flight airline business*.

Kamble, R., & Deepali, S. (2018). Applications of Artificial Intelligence in Human Life. *International Journal of Research – Granthaalayah, 6*(6).
[http://dx.doi.org/10.29121/granthaalayah.v6.i6.2018.1363]

Karbassi Yazdi, A., Spulbar, C., Hanne, T., Birau, R. (2022). Ranking performance indicators related to banking by using hybrid multicriteria methods in an uncertain environment: a case study for Iran under COVID-19 conditions. *Syst. Sci. Control Eng., 10*(1), 166-180.
[http://dx.doi.org/10.1080/21642583.2022.2052996]

Kaur, N., Sahdev, S.L., Sharma, M., Siddiqui, L. Banking 4.0: "The Influence of Artificial Intelligence on the Banking Industry & How AI is Changing the Face of Modern Day. Banks". *Int. J. Manag., 11*(6), 577-585. Available from: http://iaeme.com/Home/issue/IJM?Volume=11&Issue=6. (2020).
[http://dx.doi.org/10.34218/IJM.11.6.2020.049]

Koerselman, N. (2023). The Impact of AI on the Banking Industry. Available from: http://essay.utwente.nl/96252/1/Research_The_Impact_of_AI_on_the_Banking_Industry.pdf.

Kumar, M. (2018). Understanding Genetic Algorithms in the Artificial Intelligence Spectrum, Available from: https://medium.com/.

Lieder, F., Griffiths, T.L., M Huys, Q.J., Goodman, N.D. (2018). The anchoring bias reflects rational use of cognitive resources. *Psychon. Bull. Rev., 25*(1), 322-349.
[http://dx.doi.org/10.3758/s13423-017-1286-8] [PMID: 28484952]

Lu, J., Wu, D., Mao, M., Wang, W., Zhang, G. (2015). Recommender system application developments: A survey. *Decis. Support Syst., 74*, 12-32.
[http://dx.doi.org/10.1016/j.dss.2015.03.008]

Malali, A.B., Gopalakrishnan, S. (2020). Application of artifcial intelligence and its powered technologies in the indian banking and fnancial industry: An overview. *IOSR Journal of Humanities and Social Science, 25*(4), 55-60.

Mehrotra, A. (2019). Artifcial Intelligence in Financial Services–Need to Blend Automation with Human Touch. *International Conference on Automation, Computational and Technology Management (ICACTM)*, 342-347.

[http://dx.doi.org/10.1109/ICACTM.2019.8776741]

Noreen, U., Shafique, A., Ahmed, Z., Ashfaq, M. (2023). Banking 4.0: AI in Banking Industry & Consumer's Perspective. *Sustainability, 15*(4), 3682.
[http://dx.doi.org/10.3390/su15043682]

O'Brien, A. J. (2000). Introduction to Information Systems, Essentials for the Internetworked Enterprise. 9/d., McGraw-Hill/ Irwin Inc.

Palaniappan, V. (2018). Introduction to Neural Networks for Finance. Analytics Vidhya. Available from: https://medium.com/analytics-vidhya/introduction-to-neural-networks-for-finance-6abd5675e497.

Petropoulos, G. (2018). The impact of artificial intelligence on employment. *Praise for Work in the Digital Age*, 119.

Shawar, B. and Atwell, E. (2007). Chatbots: Are they Really Useful?. *LDV Forum, 22*, 29-49.

Shaw, J., Rudzicz, F., Jamieson, T., Goldfarb, A. (2019). Artificial intelligence and the implementation challenge. *J. Med. Internet Res., 21*(7), e13659.
[http://dx.doi.org/10.2196/13659] [PMID: 31293245]

Shi, Z. (2019). Advanced artificial intelligence. *World Scientific, 4*.

Stanra Tech Solusions PvT Ltd. (2023). Benefits of AI in Banking and Finance. Available from: https://www.linkedin.com/pulse/benefits-ai-banking-finance-stanra-tech-solutions.

Shapira B, Ricci F, Kantor PB, Rokach L (2011). Recommender systems handbook. Springer, New York.

Tang, S.M., Tien, H.N. (2020). Impact of Artificial Intelligence on Vietnam Commercial Bank Operations. *International Journal of Social Science and Economics Invention, 6*(7), 296-303.
[http://dx.doi.org/10.23958/ijssei/vol06-i07/216]

Tarafdar, M., Beath, C.M., Ross, J.W. (2019). Using AI to enhance business operations. *MIT Sloan Manag. Rev., 60*(4), 37-44.

Tuomi, I. (2018). The Impact of Artificial Intelligence on Learning, Teaching, and Education. Policies for the future, Eds. Cabrera, M., Vuorikari, R & Punie, Y., EUR 29442 EN, Publications Office of the European Union, Luxembourg, ISBN 978-92-79-97257-7, JRC113226.
[http://dx.doi.org/10.2760/12297]

CHAPTER 5

The Impact of Blockchain Technology on the Banking Sector

Jayadatta Shreepada[1,*], **Mohammed Majeed**[2], **Jonas Yomboi**[3] and **Abdul-Razak Abubakari**[4]

[1] *Department of Marketing Management, KLE's Institute of Management Studies and Research (IMSR), BVB Campus, Vidyanagar, Hubli, Karnataka State, India*

[2] *Marketing Department, Tamale Technical University, Tamale, Ghana*

[3] *Accountancy Department, Valley View University, Oyibi-Ghana*

[4] *Entrepreneurship and Enterprise Development, Tamale Technical University, Tamale, Ghana*

Abstract: Blockchain technology is primarily an internet-based technology that exhibits significant potential to bring about transformative advancements across various domains. This technology has the potential to completely revolutionise the banking business and its services. Therefore, the chapter aimed to elucidate the utilisation of Blockchain (BC) inside the financial services and how it Impacts on the banking sector. The potential outcomes of this development encompass enhanced efficacy, heightened security, and increased openness within the financial system. Moreover, there exists the possibility of the emergence of novel applications of blockchain-based technologies, which might potentially lead to a paradigm shift in our conceptualization of finance and economics. The authors explore how advancements in technology will impact transaction processes within the global banking system. Specifically, they investigate the integration of these digital currencies into existing transaction systems, highlighting the role of technologies like blockchain in enhancing the efficiency and effectiveness of the global banking system. This integration aims to achieve a fully decentralised, distributed, transparent, fast, immutable, and efficient banking system.

Keywords: Blockchain, Banking, Cryptocurrencies, Distributed, Decentralized, Financial, Immutable.

INTRODUCTION

The contemporary banking sector is confronted with various concerns, including escalating operational expenses, heightened vulnerability to malicious assaults on

* **Corresponding author Jayadatta Shreepada:** Department of Marketing Management, KLE's Institute of Management Studies and Research (IMSR), BVB Campus, Vidyanagar, Hubli, Karnataka State, India; E-mail: jayadattaster@gmail.com

centralised servers, and difficulties in ensuring transparency. This is primarily due to the fact that a significant portion of banking transactions, such as customer account openings and global payments, often involve labor-intensive manual processing and extensive documentation. Additionally, these activities typically require the involvement of expensive suppliers and are time-consuming, as they must be confirmed by multiple participants at different stages. Consequently, this process often leads to delays and a lack of real-time solutions that are resistant to fraud (Delloitte, 2017). Therefore, financial institutions are consistently seeking novel methods to expedite transaction processes in order to improve customer service, while simultaneously prioritising cost-effectiveness and maintaining transparency for both customers and regulatory bodies (Delloitte, 2017). Blockchain has the potential to offer a solution for banks due to its intrinsic ability to eliminate intermediaries, keep an immutable record of transactions, and enable real-time transaction execution. The implementation of this approach has the ability to mitigate the risk associated with banking transactions, resulting in decreased expenses related to manual labour, and ultimately leading to improved customer service and satisfaction. The relationship between blockchain and financial technology (FinTech) is intimate, given the frequent utilisation of blockchain technology in many FinTech applications. FinTech encompasses the utilisation of technological advancements to enhance and revolutionise financial services, including but not limited to mobile payments, online banking, and investment management. This offers numerous opportunities and prospects within the Finance and FinTech sector. The operational processes within the banking industry exhibit characteristics of repetitiveness, time consumption, and high costs. In order to address these challenges, prominent financial institutions, including central banks, are actively investigating the potential applications of blockchain technology within their current operational framework. Banks are actively pursuing strategies to achieve a substantial reduction in back-office operational expenses. Fintech start-ups, leveraging cutting-edge technology such as blockchain, are presenting a formidable challenge to traditional banks by offering services that are characterised by enhanced speed, transparency, and cost-effectiveness. They have successfully acquired substantial market shares within the payment industry. Given the intensifying competitive landscape, the significance of blockchain technology has become paramount for banks worldwide. According to Casey, Crane, Gensler, Johnson, and Narula (2018), in the context of the finance sector, this technological advancement would facilitate the secure and dependable movement of currency. Furthermore, the implementation of this technology has been found to enhance security measures and mitigate the potential for fraudulent activities, while expediting and optimising financial operations (Storm2, 2023). The integration of blockchain technology inside the FinTech sector holds significant promise for transformative effects on the financial industry. Numerous FinTech enterprises are actively investigating the use of blockchain in their offerings and operations. Blockchain technology has exhibited significant disruptive effects in the financial sector, demonstrating its capacity to fundamentally transform corporate operations. In order to comprehend the potential impact of Blockchain and cryptocurrencies on the global banking system, it is imperative to possess a comprehensive understanding of the functioning of the financial system, encompassing both classic and contemporary approaches. Additionally, it is imperative to ascertain the necessity of implementing Blockchain technology within the financial sector and examine the revitalising impact of cryptocurrencies on the entirety of the banking system. According to Dhanda (2022), banks are financial institutions that are operated by centralised governing authorities inside a certain country. The bank assumes responsibility for facilitating transactions between multiple parties, regardless of their direct or independent relationship with one another. The Indian banking system encompasses five distinct categories of banks, namely the central bank, commercial bank, investment bank, cooperative bank, and postal bank (Dhanda, 2022). The banks offer a range of services encompassing retail banking, personal banking, commercial banking, investment banking, credit and debit facilities, online banking, loan provision, insurance management, and mutual fund services, among others (Yomboi *et al.*, 2021). The banking system comprises three fundamental components, namely capital, deposits, and loans. In its inception, the concept of the banking system entailed the practice of individuals engaging in the movement of funds between different accounts. When the surge of interest in blockchain commenced a few years ago, there was a considerable level of anticipation over its potential applications. The potential of blockchain technology was widely promoted as a means to address the challenges faced by various sectors, including supply chains, finance, healthcare, and democratic systems. However, the outcomes of experiments done on prospective applications of blockchain, such as pilot programmes carried out in the financial services and banking sector, did not meet these expectations. As a result, the industry's enthusiasm for blockchain use cases diminished (Portilla *et al.*, 2022). In several instances, individuals with an interest in blockchain technology have discovered that conventional, centralised databases possess the capacity to offer equivalent capabilities as blockchain, albeit at a reduced expense. Blockchain technology has emerged as a prominent tool within the financial technology (fintech) sector, finding widespread utilisation. Moreover, it has been seen that banks can get advantageous outcomes from the adoption of this technology (Sharma, 2020). Hence, the chapter sought to unveil how Blockchain (BC) works in the finance and banking sector.

Contribution

The primary focus of this chapter entails conducting a comprehensive literature review on the most recent advancements in blockchain banking. The chapter encompasses an examination of significant instances of banking innovation, such as openness, safety, rapidity, and cost saving. These cases provide valuable strategic insights for forecasting the advancement and dissemination of technology in the context of blockchain technology banking.

LITERATURE REVIEW

Blockchain

The data is maintained within a centralised repository and distributed throughout a worldwide ledger with sophisticated cryptographic techniques. When a transaction occurs, miners leverage their substantial computational resources to construct a block within approximately 10 minutes. This block incorporates all preceding transactions (Sharma, 2020). According to Zhang and Zhang (2022), the utilisation of technology enables numerous key nodes within an information system to employ a series of cryptographic techniques. This allows for the potential correlation of data blocks, each of which encompasses all pertinent details of transactions for a specific effective system time. Additionally, this technology generates data to authenticate the truthfulness of other records and serves as a connection to the subsequent data block. Blockchain technology serves as the underlying infrastructure and mechanism for documenting Bitcoin transactions, thereby enabling the potential for recording a wide range of information. According to Gupta (2018, pp. 3-6), Blockchain has a multitude of attributes that have the potential to address challenges across several domains. Blockchain possesses two primary attributes: decentralisation and immutability. Blockchain technology operates in a decentralised manner, wherein the records are dispersed among multiple parties instead of being stored in a central ledger. The system enables the establishment of a decentralised communication network among peers, thereby obviating the necessity for intermediaries. The technology known as blockchain, which serves as the foundation for cryptocurrencies, has the potential to have a transformative impact on the global economy. The concept of blockchain entails a decentralised ledger system. The system has the capability to retain factual information pertaining to land ownership or bond ownership. According to Sankaranarayanan (2020), the utilisation of technology allows for the establishment of an unalterable record of ownership and facilitates the transfer of assets among parties who lack trust in one another. The advent of blockchain technology has led to the emergence of digital currencies, with Bitcoin being a notable illustration. Furthermore, it finds application in the monitoring of ownership pertaining to various assets, including stocks and bonds. The utilisation of blockchain technology has undergone a transformation over the course of time, resulting in a diverse range of applications, including but not limited to cryptocurrencies, supply chain management, and voting systems (Storm2, 2023). The aforementioned technology possesses the significant potential to disrupt several businesses through its capacity to mitigate fraudulent activities, enhance transparency, and optimise operational efficiency. The removal of the third party results in increased efficiency and cost-effectiveness of the operation. Another noteworthy characteristic is immutability, which refers to the inability to alter a recorded transaction once it has been finalised. If there is a need to update the transaction, a new transaction is generated and disseminated over all networks for updating purposes. The verification of transactions is conducted by other computers inside the network, ensuring their integrity and preventing any potential tampering. Therefore, it offers a heightened level of security and reliability (Attaran & Gunasekaran, 2019).

Blockchain in Finance and Banking

Blockchain technology is characterised by its decentralised and distributed nature, serving as a ledger for recording transactions across several computers. This design ensures that any retroactive revision of the record necessitates the modification of all following blocks and the consensus of the network (Ulatus, 2022). Blockchain is a decentralised technology that employs a distributed ledger system to store encrypted blocks containing digital transaction records executed by participants in the blockchain network. When blockchain technology is employed as a business network, it facilitates the ability of participants to document their transactions and subsequently monitor them within the system. According to Baranowska (2021), it is not possible to delete or alter the recorded transactions within the block. In this manner, the utilisation of blockchain technology facilitates users' enhancement of the security, reliability, transparency, and efficiency of financial processes. This technology facilitates the enhancement of data safety by rendering it unchangeable and facilitating ease of verification. The implementation of this technology has the potential to significantly enhance data security across many businesses, thereby mitigating the risks associated with fraudulent activities and errors. The banking industry is particularly vulnerable to fraudulent activities, making the adoption of blockchain technology in financial services a potential solution to mitigate these risks. The financial and banking industries are experiencing a growing use of blockchains, primarily driven by their inherent benefits of immutability, transparency, and enhanced security. Blockchain technology has the capacity to facilitate the recording of transactions between two entities in a manner that is both verifiable and enduring. This feature is particularly advantageous in situations where there is a requirement for precise and unalterable documentation of transactions. One potential use of blockchains is their utilisation in the recording and settlement of trades, management of financial assets, facilitation of payment processing, and establishment of secure smart contracts involving many entities. Furthermore, the utilisation of blockchain technology facilitates transparency by virtue of its inherent feature of publicly accessible transaction history recorded on the ledger (Ulatus, 2022). This facilitates the provision of information to all parties involved, allowing them to have a clear understanding of ongoing actions and mitigating the potential for fraudulent behaviour. As a result, the implementation of blockchains in the financial and banking industries has yielded numerous advantages, leading to a growing adoption of this technology by organisations operating within this sector.

The banking industry constitutes a significant portion of the global economy. Banks are often recognised as the largest and most established financial intermediaries on a global scale. The advent of digitalization has significantly influenced the banking sector, resulting in a profound transformation of the overall banking system. The barter system was rendered obsolete with the introduction of commodity money, which then gave way to fiat money. Presently, digital currency and digital payment methods have taken precedence (Attaran & Gunasekaran, 2019). Over time, advancements in technology have enabled the provision of many financial services to users, including automated teller machines (ATMs), electronic cash transfers, electronic clearing services, real-time gross settlement systems, internet banking platforms, debit and credit cards, and mobile banking applications. Currently, the banking business heavily relies on technology, and as such, blockchain has the potential to significantly alter the landscape of this sector. Blockchain technology enables the immutable recording of transactions within blocks. The removal of third parties is observed. The concept of blockchain has the potential to bring about significant changes in the banking and financial industries. The technology possesses the capacity to cause a substantial transformation in the financial sector. According to Gupta and Gupta (2018), the distinctive attribute of blockchain technology is advantageous in the finance sector due to its capacity to safely and transparently record transactions (Storm2, 2023). A platform for truth and trust is constituted by an immutable and unhackable distributed ledger of digital assets. The conclusions have significant ramifications not only within the financial services business but also across several societal domains (Sankaranarayanan, 2020). The concept of blockchain refers to the storage of digital information within a publicly accessible database. The technology typically encompasses cryptocurrencies and offers enhanced security for a range of financial operations, hence becoming a prevalent technology within the fintech industry (Sharma, 2022). As previously stated, blockchains function as databases. Blockchain technology consists of a series of transaction blocks that are interconnected through cryptographic means. The blocks contain data pertaining to the entities participating in a transaction as well. As an illustration, blockchain technology is capable of documenting a transaction devoid of any personally identifiable information, opting instead to employ a digital signature. Blockchain technology not only retains data but also incorporates distinguishing attributes that set it apart from other forms of data storage. The system will retain a distinct alphanumeric identifier, known as a hash, which facilitates the categorization of individual units of data (Attaran & Gunasekaran, 2019). Blockchain technology enables banks to securely store and record transactional data pertaining to several aspects, including the precise date, time, and monetary value of recent purchases. Additionally, this technology enables the participants to efficiently check and audit transactions at a low cost. A blockchain is composed of a sequence of blocks, whereby each block contains a cryptographic hash of the preceding block, a timestamp, and transaction data. The inherent nature of a blockchain is such that it exhibits resistance to any attempts to modify the data contained inside it.

Benefits of BC in the Financial Services

The utilisation of distributed ledger technologies offers numerous advantages for the financial services industry. The implementation of blockchain technology facilitates decentralisation, enabling banks to allocate their resources towards additional endeavours beyond the mere monitoring of payment transactions. The implementation of blockchain technology has brought about significant transformations in the financial sector across various dimensions. The advent of this technology has had a significant impact on various aspects of financial operations, including but not limited to systems for payments, settlement processes, fundraising activities, securities administration, loan management, credit operations, and trade finance. The utilisation of blockchain technology in payment systems enables decentralised ledgers, which in turn facilitate speedier payment processing and reduced transaction fees compared to traditional banking institutions. The implementation of blockchain technology has a significant impact on clearance and settlement systems, as it leverages distributed ledgers to effectively minimise operational costs and facilitate real-time transactions across financial institutions.

Capital Markets

Capital markets refer to the financial markets where individuals, businesses, and governments can raise funds by buying and selling various financial instruments. The utilisation of blockchain technology possesses significant potential in revolutionising the existing capital market trading mechanism. The capital market is characterised by a complex and time-consuming process for settling financial transactions. Capital markets encompass a diverse array of intermediaries, including predominantly investment banks, brokers, investors, and credit agencies, among others, who actively engage in market activities. Currently, the individuals involved in this process maintain their ledger and execute the necessary modifications. This method is both time-consuming and costly. According to Gupta and Gupta (2018), a prevailing issue within the capital market pertains to the existence of diverse clearing and settlement methods. Due to the involvement of multiple parties, the counterparty risk associated with this situation is elevated. The act of defaulting by a single party has the potential to exert a significant influence on the entire market. The process frequently exhibits a lack of speed and effectiveness (Petrov, 2019).

Decentralisation

Decentralisation refers to the process of redistributing power, authority, and decision-making. Decentralisation is a prominent attribute of blockchain technology that holds significant relevance within the financial domain. The implementation of decentralisation fosters a heightened level of democratic interaction within the market, facilitating a more equitable relationship between individuals and institutions. According to Baranowska (2021), rather than depending on a centralised authority that exercises control over all transactions, individuals engaging in transactions have the ability to directly speak with one another. Consequently, this phenomenon leads to reduced operating expenditures, heightened confidence among participants, and the prevention of market manipulation by people or distinct entities.

Disintermediation

Disintermediation refers to the process of eliminating intermediaries in a supply chain or distribution. The utilisation of blockchain technology offers the advantages of transaction immutability and a distributed ledger architecture, both of which are essential components in the elimination of the necessity for a trusted intermediary in the ecosystem. The utilisation of tamper-proof distributed data creates an atmosphere where trust is not a concern, facilitating counterparties to engage in operations with the assurance that they possess an identical and unmodifiable version of the truth, along with its complete historical record.

Minimising Expenses

The use of blockchain technology presents significant advantages in terms of reduced transaction costs and time efficiency. However, it is important to acknowledge that the initial investment required for adopting this technology may be substantial, and the amount of time required to recoup this investment may also be lengthy. One of the advantages that blockchain technology offers banks is the potential for cost reduction. According to Sharma (2022), banks have lately discovered that the implementation of blockchain technology has the potential to significantly decrease their infrastructure expenses by as much as $20 billion by the year 2022. Therefore, financial institutions must take into account the long-term investment outlook and ensure that the investment aligns with their stated vision statement (Delloitte, 2017). By incorporating technologies such as smart contracts into their platforms, banks have the potential to minimise their engagement with counterparties and intermediaries. Additionally, they have the potential to reduce the expenses associated with the upkeep and implementation of contracts. According to Gupta (2018), there is a trend among investors to shift away from financial advisors in order to circumvent the imposition of elevated fees. In this context, the use of blockchain technology presents a potential avenue for consumers to avail themselves of reduced expenses linked to conventional financial services. Financial technology (fintech) firms have emerged as a significant component of the financial services sector, facilitating the ability of investors to establish accounts with digital advisors and exercise autonomous financial choices. As the fintech industry continues to exert a greater influence on the global financial landscape, its association with blockchain technology is expected to grow inescapably.

Transparency

The concept of transparency refers to the quality or state of being open, clear, and easily understood. The implementation of blockchain technology within the banking sector enhances transaction transparency, facilitating the identification and mitigation of fraudulent activities. The utilisation of a shared digital ledger by banks for the purpose of documenting transactions results in an enhanced level of visibility for the participants of the blockchain (Baranowska, 2021). Hence, financial institutions have the capability to effectively monitor the chronological record of individual transactions and authenticate them. Blockchain banking eliminates the possibility of money laundering, fraudulent activities, and deceptive operations. The implementation of blockchain technology will greatly enhance transparency among market participants. The system utilises standardised protocols, mutualized standards, and shared processes, functioning as a unified and authoritative source of information for all members within the network. Blockchain implementations facilitate the establishment of a publicly accessible and contemporaneous record of activities within a certain ecosystem, which is available to all participants in the market. Enhanced levels of openness inside financial institutions have been observed to result in greater regulatory reporting and monitoring by central banks, particularly when regulators are granted access to blockchain technology (Baranowska, 2021). The significance of transparency has grown in tandem with the expansion of transaction capabilities. The conventional banking system is known for its high level of confidentiality, but blockchain technology offers a potential solution to enhance transparency and security in the banking process. By utilising blockchain, records are securely stored, and users can access comprehensive historical data. Additionally, blockchain allows for the possibility of granting authorised parties exclusive access to shared transaction ledgers (Hillsberg, 2018). Furthermore, it should be noted that any modifications carried out on public blockchains are readily accessible to all participants, as stated by Ho (2016). According to Tapscott and Tapscott (2016), it is evident that blockchain technology has the potential to reduce or remove reliance on trust in transactions, while also facilitating transparent and real-time auditing processes. Furthermore, the potential of blockchain technology extends beyond the automation of financial reporting (Collomb & Sok, 2016). The inherent transparency of blockchain facilitates real-time communication between banks and regulators, enabling prompt intervention in cases of compliance breaches (Patel, 2018). In the absence of blockchain technology, individual organisations are required to maintain distinct databases. Due to the utilisation of a distributed ledger, blockchain technology ensures that transactions and data are consistently recorded across many locations in a similar manner. All individuals who are granted authorised access to the network are able to view identical information simultaneously, ensuring complete transparency. All transactions are recorded in an immutable manner, with each transaction being assigned a specific time and date stamp. According to IBM (2023), this feature allows users to access the complete transaction history, effectively mitigating the possibility of fraudulent activities. According to Ganatra (2022), people engage in activities on a publicly accessible ledger with the use of blockchain technology. Consequently, the industry is experiencing an increased level of transparency. Transparency can play a crucial role in identifying inefficiencies and facilitating problem-solving, thereby mitigating risks for financial institutions.

Smart Contracts

Smart contracts refer to self-executing agreements with the terms of the agreement directly written into code. Contracts in the financial domain are intricate and require a significant investment of time. According to Marr (2017), the use of blockchains enables the establishment of smart contracts through the implementation and storage of computer codes. These codes can be run to generate contracts or authorise financial transactions, contingent upon the input of keys by two or more parties and the fulfillment of specific predetermined criteria. According to Accenture Technology Vision (2018) research, a significant majority of CEOs surveyed, specifically 60%, expressed the belief that blockchain technology and smart contracts would hold utmost importance in the forthcoming three decades.

Efficient Processes

The implementation of advanced automation technologies leads to a significant enhancement in the overall efficiency of operations. The implementation of this technology facilitates immediate settlement as well as enhances the ability to conduct audits and generate reports in real-time. Moreover, it significantly diminishes processing durations, the likelihood of errors and delays, and the reliance on several steps and intermediaries that are typically necessary to attain comparable levels of assurance in conventional procedures.

Enhancing Capital Optimisation

One of the primary characteristics of blockchain technology is its ability to eliminate the necessity for a trusted intermediary, thereby enabling peer-to-peer transactions. The implementation of blockchain technology inside the financial services sector has the potential to render fee-charging intermediaries, such as custodial banks and clearers, obsolete (Ganatra, 2022). Blockchain technology provides enhanced capital optimisation by significantly reducing operational expenses for banks. Furthermore, the collective expenses associated with implementing and maintaining a shared blockchain among banks may surpass the individual costs incurred by each bank in administering their own transaction processes. Nevertheless, the expenses are distributed among all the institutions involved, resulting in a substantial reduction in expenditures.

Automation

The concept of automation refers to the use of technology and machinery to perform tasks and processes. Transactions can also be automated through the use of "smart contracts," enhancing efficiency and expediting the process. The impact of blockchain technology extends beyond the realm of money transactions within the banking industry. The utilisation of technology offers significant advantages in the monitoring and recording of transactions, presenting the potential for streamlined automation. Smart contracts enable financial service providers to effectively monitor and record buyer payments and seller deliverables. Furthermore, it has the capability to effectively resolve any issues that may develop during the course of the transaction. According to Ganatra (2022), the implementation of automated systems has been found to decrease the likelihood of human error. Upon the fulfillment of predetermined criteria, the subsequent phase of a transaction or process is initiated automatically. According to IBM (2023), the implementation of smart contracts serves to minimise human involvement and diminish the need for external entities to validate the fulfillment of contractual obligations. In the context of insurance, it is worth noting that with the completion of the required documentation by a customer to initiate a claim, the claim may be promptly resolved and remunerated through an automated process.

The Mitigation of Counterparty Risks

The near-instant settlement of transactions mitigates the risk associated with counterparty default, hence reducing potential financial liabilities for banks.

Tokenization

Tokenization is the process of dividing a sequence of text into smaller units, known as tokens. The process of tokenization involves converting assets and financial instruments into programmable units, thereby simplifying their management and facilitating their trading activities. Tokenization enables broader market access by facilitating enhanced connectivity and the potential for fractional ownership. As a consequence, there is a rise in the level of liquidity and a decline in the cost of capital.

Traceability

The concept of traceability refers to the ability to track and document history and location. The utilisation of blockchain technology facilitates the establishment of an audit trail, which effectively records and certifies the origin and subsequent movements of an item throughout its entire trajectory. In sectors where consumers express apprehension regarding environmental or human rights implications associated with a product, or in industries grappling with the challenges of counterfeiting and fraudulent activities, this evidence serves to substantiate claims. The utilisation of blockchain technology enables the direct dissemination of provenance-related information to customers. Traceability data has the potential to reveal vulnerabilities within a supply chain, such as the presence of products that are left unattended on a loading dock while awaiting transportation.

Enhanced Contractual Performance

The utilisation of smart contracts by banks and financial institutions is expected to enhance the fulfillment of contractual terms. This improvement stems from the automatic execution of smart contracts upon the fulfillment of predetermined circumstances. Ensuring that smart contracts are securely grounded in legal frameworks and adhere to regulatory requirements, even across many jurisdictions if necessary, is of utmost significance. As a result, R3CEV was compelled to customise the smart contracts integrated into their distributed ledger platform. Blockchain technology can offer significant advantages to intricate financial asset transactions, mostly attributed to its ability to facilitate automatic settlement through the utilisation of smart contracts governed by an incorruptible set of business rules.

Enhanced Efficiency in Service Delivery

One further benefit of implementing blockchain technology in the banking sector is the provision of expedited transaction processing. According to Sharma (2022), it is possible to complete any transaction within a brief timeframe, with a modest advantage in speed compared to conventional techniques. Banks have developed the capability to bypass intermediaries, enabling them to expedite consumer transactions. This will lead to an increased capacity for customers and banks to carry out and facilitate a greater number of transactions. Conventional procedures that heavily rely on paper documentation are characterised by their protracted duration, susceptibility to human fallibility, and frequent dependence on intermediaries. By implementing blockchain technology, the efficiency and speed of transactions can be significantly enhanced. The storage of documentation on the blockchain, in conjunction with transaction details, obviates the necessity for paper-based exchanges. According to IBM (2023), the reconciliation of numerous ledgers is unnecessary, hence enabling expedited clearing and settlement processes. Currently, numerous banking activities and financial transactions exhibit a notable lack of efficiency, resulting in prolonged durations for their administration, authorization, and documentation. Furthermore, certain tasks continue to be executed by hand. The utilisation of fintech blockchain effectively addresses this problem by enabling immediate authentication and verification, thereby facilitating the optimisation of banking operations such as expedited cross-border payments, financial trading, and KYC verification. This technology also contributes to the reduction of paperwork (Baranowska, 2021).

Provenance

The term "provenance" refers to the origin or source of something, particularly in data. Blockchain technology ensures the preservation of an unalterable ledger of transactions, thereby establishing and preserving the ownership of assets from the moment they are initially involved in a transaction recorded on the blockchain. This leads to a substantial decrease in risk and the necessity for related mitigating actions for various types of assets. This skill has the potential to effectively mitigate instances of theft, fraud, and misrepresentation pertaining to valuable assets and intellectual property. Additionally, the establishment of a digital footprint on the blockchain can be advantageous for goods whose value is contingent upon their provenance.

Augmentation of Financial Solutions

The availability of a broader range of financial solutions during periods of economic turmoil has been enhanced by the emergence of cryptocurrencies, digital currencies, and tokens. Following the occurrence of the Bitfinex hack, the company devised a resolution strategy that involved providing compensation to its consumers. This compensation took the form of a tradeable Recovery Right Token (RRT), which was distributed evenly among all affected customers, ensuring an equitable distribution of the incurred losses. Each individual token possessed a monetary value of $1 in deficit and thus might be perceived as a promissory note. Customers have the option to engage in token trading at the prevailing market price, either due to their lack of confidence in Bitfinex's recovery or their desire to generate profits. Alternatively, customers may opt to exchange the token for equity, a course of action pursued by approximately half of all token holders. Lastly, Bitfinex retains the option to repurchase the tokens from customers at a future date for a fixed price of $1. Following an initial decline in value, the RRT has had a subsequent increase in price, currently trading at approximately $0.80. Furthermore, Bitfinex has resumed its normal operations. The blockchain has facilitated the development of a noteworthy financial solution that showcases innovation. According to Sankaranarayanan (2020), the absence of the mentioned entity would have significantly increased the probability of Bitfinex facing insolvency, resulting in the complete loss of funds for its clientele.

Enhanced Security Measures

The utilisation of blockchain technology in the banking sector enables organisations to address a diverse array of security concerns. According to Baranowska (2021), the use of technology can span many levels, including the safeguarding of sensitive documents as well as the enhancement of user authentication. The utilisation of blockchain technology in the banking sector can provide heightened levels of security for financial data. This is mostly due to the inherent immutability of historical information within the blockchain, which prevents any unauthorised alterations. Additionally, the real-time addition of new information is shared among numerous entities, further increasing the difficulty of data manipulation (Garcia, 2018b; Harsono, 2018). According to Patel (2018), the modification of data within a block may be effectively monitored and recorded to mitigate instances of fraud and misuse. Furthermore, the utilisation of blockchain technology enables prompt communication and updates regarding suspected fraudulent activities. The utilisation of shared ledgers has the potential to enhance the security of transaction information within the banking sector. According to Guta (2018), one advantage of utilising this method is the ability to expedite transactions, hence mitigating the potential risks associated with unauthorised access to transaction data or fraudulent diversion of payments. Each transaction is associated with a pair of security keys. In the context of cryptographic systems, it is common for each user to own a public key, which is accessible to all parties involved, and a private key, which is only shared amongst the relevant participants in a specific transaction. Once a transaction has been validated, the data associated with it becomes immutable. With the growing engagement of consumers in online activities, the digital realm has emerged as a fertile environment for fraudulent individuals. The implementation of blockchain technology has the potential to mitigate this particular risk. According to Gupta *et al.* (2018), transactions and monetary transfers conducted on the blockchain exhibit enhanced speed and traceability compared to conventional banking systems. The transmission of information *via* several financial intermediaries entails a potential vulnerability wherein the interception of said information may occur, hence increasing the likelihood of fraudulent activities. The existing gap in supervision can be effectively addressed by leveraging the cryptographic algorithms of blockchain technology, which enhance the security of information exchange among involved parties.

The implementation of blockchain technology obviates the need for safeguarding user and bank accounts as well as devices through the utilisation of passwords. In contrast, the technology integrates the robust security of blockchain with the utilisation of biometrics, thereby encrypting the distinctive identifiers of users, such as iris scans, fingerprints, speech patterns, and so on, within a block on the blockchain. The technology employs encrypted blocks containing user IDs as access keys for applications and devices, or as keys for digitally signing the data transmitted by the user to other parties (Baranowska, 2021). The decentralised structure of blockchain necessitates that cyber thieves engage with the entirety of the blockchain system rather than a singular central node in order to perpetrate hacking activities. Given the distribution of data over several nodes, there is no specific server or location that can be targeted for an attack. Due to this rationale, several financial institutions employ blockchain technology for the purpose of data preservation and ensuring the security of transactions (Baranowska, 2021). The utilisation of blockchain technology can effectively enhance the security of internal communication systems, hence mitigating the risks associated with data leakages and cyber espionage. The technique facilitates the dissemination of metadata employed in communication across a distributed ledger, hence rendering it unfeasible for hackers to aggregate said metadata at a single centralised location.

Enhanced Data Quality

Contemporary blockchain technology possesses the capability to securely store diverse forms of data and facilitate its retrieval in accordance with predetermined protocols and guidelines. Smart contracts are a technological innovation that facilitates the automatic verification and enforcement of contractual agreements. By transferring banking data onto distributed ledgers, the data subsequently acquires the advantages associated with blockchain technology.

Securitization

Securitization refers to the process of transforming illiquid assets into tradable securities. The utilisation of blockchain technology in the realm of structured finance is facilitated through a mechanism referred to as "tokenisation" (Storm2, 2023). The process of tokenization involves the conversion of commonly illiquid assets owned by a special purpose vehicle (SPV) into "tokens." These tokens serve as representations of the individual securities that are then sold to investors on the blockchain. According to Harris and Wonglimpiyarat (2019), the aforementioned tokens will subsequently be allocated to each respective investor, serving as evidence of their ownership of each specific asset. The potential of blockchain technology lies in its ability to tokenize conventional securities, including stocks, bonds, and alternative assets, and then integrate them into public blockchains. This integration has the potential to enhance the efficiency and interoperability of capital markets.

Cryptocurrencies

Digital currencies, often known as cryptocurrencies, are a form of digital or virtual money that utilise cryptography for secure transactions and control its creation. The utilisation of digital currency in conjunction with blockchain technology can provide advantageous outcomes for banks. Currently, they possess the capability to embrace digital currency as a means to carry out a diverse range of transactions. The implementation of cryptocurrencies will facilitate enhanced efficiency and security in the clearing and settlement of financial trades by banks.

Syndicated Loans

Syndicated loans are financial instruments commonly utilised in the corporate sector, whereby a group of lenders collectively provide funds to a borrower. It is anticipated that the utilisation of smart contracts to regulate loan terms and conditions, distributed ledger technology to address communication and transaction tracking, as well as transparency and immutable data to alleviate time-consuming reconciliations and erroneous payments, will enhance the efficiency of execution and servicing within the syndicated loan ecosystem.

Accountability

Accountability refers to the state or quality of being responsible for one's actions, and decisions. By implementing accountability measures, financial institutions can leverage blockchain technology to mitigate instances of fraud and unauthorised utilisation of corporate resources, thereby achieving advantageous outcomes. According to Pratt (2023), the implementation of digitally generated transactions in banking operations eliminates the concern of encountering substantial errors. There will be no concern over the fabrication of crucial facts. The implementation of blockchain technology facilitates the seamless verification and auditing of all transactions, hence enhancing the accuracy and consistency of transaction processing within the banking sector.

Streamline and Monitor the Movement of Data

The objective is to streamline and monitor the movement of data inside a financial organisation.

While blockchain technology has been well recognised for its ability to facilitate trust among various organisations, financial institutions are increasingly leveraging it to foster trust inside their own departments. According to Pratt (2023), pioneers in the field of blockchain have observed a rise in the use of blockchain technology within organisations. This is primarily attributed to the benefits it provides in terms of facilitating the transfer of intra-company data, safeguarding customer data, and ensuring compliance with regulatory obligations.

Compliance

The concept of compliance refers to the act of conforming to rules, regulations, or guidelines. Banks stand to gain advantages in terms of enhanced compliance through the implementation of blockchain technology. Access to the blockchain can be granted to auditors and government officials. Through this level of access, auditors and governmental entities are able to observe the operations of businesses with the utmost openness. Financial institutions have the capability to detect and intercept potentially fraudulent transactional behaviour, hence enhancing the efficiency of auditing procedures. Financial institutions, including fintech firms, have the capacity to offer digital information that is readily accessible and facilitates efficiency in the auditing process. The significance of regulatory compliance has witnessed a notable rise within the realms of commerce and finance. Ensuring compliance with laws, rules, and regulations related to their activities is vital for financial institutions. Firms face significant difficulties in effectively managing the rapid and intricate nature of regulatory modifications, especially when operating internationally and being subject to many regulatory frameworks.

Ultimately, blockchain technology possesses the capacity to revolutionise financial reporting and compliance. Banks and other financial institutions are obligated to regularly engage in reporting activities, including the submission of tax filings, conducting audits, and preparing other financial reports. According to Brown (2020), timely submission of reports is a legal requirement for all banks, and it holds particular significance in the context of fraud prevention and anti-money laundering efforts. The regular preparation of reports in accordance with regulations requires a significant investment of time and human resources. The implementation of blockchain technology has the potential to streamline reporting processes and yield significant time and cost savings. The implementation of blockchain technology has the potential to reduce the need for traditional paper-based documentation. The recording and updating of transactions could be automated. This would facilitate the operations of both financial institutions and regulatory bodies. The monitoring of transactions can aid efforts in combating money laundering operations. According to Petrov (2019),

Interest Payment and Settlement

The utilisation of blockchain technology offers the potential to accomplish several advantages, including real-time transaction processing, the distribution and enforcement of business rules, cost reduction through the elimination of middlemen and infrastructure simplification, less risk of data loss, and improved end-to-end transparency and predictability. According to Brown (2020), the implementation of blockchain technology has the potential to enhance the security of borrowing money and offer reduced interest rates by eliminating the requirement for gatekeepers in the loan and credit sectors. The utilisation of blockchain distributed ledger technology has the potential to enhance and expedite the process of bank transfers. Typically, an international bank transfer may take up to three days to complete. This occurs due to the necessity of navigating a complex network of middlemen, including correspondent banks and custodial services, during the transfer process. According to Baranowska (2021), financial institutions responsible for facilitating transfer procedures must adhere to the global financial system, which encompasses a wide range of participants such as traders, asset managers, and funds. Transactions can be executed within a matter of minutes or seconds; however, the process of settling these transactions now requires a time frame of up to one week. The implementation of blockchain technology enables settlements to be optimised for users, resulting in substantial time and cost savings for all parties involved. Cash, cashier's checks, and wire transfers are considered secure and reliable payment options. Nevertheless, it is important to note that cash transactions lack a traceable record, while susceptibility to forgery exists with cashier's cheques. Additionally, wire transfers can be a time-consuming process. Blockchain-based payment systems address these problems, instilling a higher level of confidence among customers. According to Ganatra (2022), the utilisation of technology facilitates the instantaneous transmission of funds between financial institutions, reducing obstacles and expediting the process of settlement. The implementation of blockchain technology in the banking sector is expected to significantly reduce the reliance on middle office and back office personnel, as transactions would be settled instantaneously. Consequently, financial institutions possess a significant impetus to investigate the potential of blockchain technology in order to enhance settlement processes. Some banks prefer to initially study internal solutions, while others prioritise exploring collaborative options among several banks.

Minimising Error Handling and Reconciliation Processes

The implementation of blockchain technology has facilitated the process of transaction reconciliation for banks. The ability to expedite transaction tracing and identify mistakes in a more prompt manner is facilitated. This capability allows individuals to identify and rectify any mistakes or inaccuracies prior to the finalisation of a transaction. Consequently, individuals will possess the necessary resources to rectify mistakes prior to their potential impact on the organisation and its clientele (Brown, 2020). One notable characteristic of blockchain technology is its inherent immutability, whereby any data that is recorded cannot be altered or modified. Real-time tracking of data captured on a blockchain enables the creation of a highly comprehensive audit trail. Therefore, it effectively eliminates the processes of mistake handling and reconciliation.

Crypto Staking

The concept of crypto staking refers to the process through which individuals or entities hold and validate digital assets within a blockchain network. Crypto staking is an emerging financial instrument facilitated by blockchain technology. It involves crypto asset holders voluntarily committing to a predetermined period of asset lock-up, thereby providing support for the functioning of a blockchain network (Pratt, 2023). Subsequently, individuals have the ability to allocate a portion of their assets as a means to participate in the validation process of novel transactions on the blockchain and subsequently append new blocks. By validating genuine transactions, individuals can acquire additional crypto assets as a reward. Conversely, if they validate fraudulent transactions, they may forfeit a portion or the entirety of their staked assets.

Enhancing Customer Experience

The majority of financial institutions have adopted blockchain technology as a means of facilitating cross-border transactions, resulting in notable efficiencies in terms of both time and cost. According to Ganatra (2022), customers have the ability to employ blockchain technology for conducting online fund transfers through mobile devices. Individuals are no longer required to physically attend a money transfer centre, endure waiting in queues, and incur transaction costs.

Other Benefits of BC in the Banking Sector

The present study focuses on the development of automatic selection standards for the construction of syndicates within programmed smart contracts. The process of converting physical documents, including agreements, contracts, and terms and conditions documents, into digital format is known as digitization. This digitization process involves utilising blockchain technology, which enables the automation of validations and checks. This information is supported by a report by Deloitte in 2017. The incorporation of technology into various aspects of society and education. The utilisation of blockchain technology enables the automated assessment and scrutiny of data for the purpose of loan underwriting. The duration of settlement periods has decreased. Blockchain technology has the potential to enable expeditious loan funding and payment settlements by utilising smart contracts to conduct various tasks in near real-time. The assurance of document immutability is ensured. The immutability feature of the blockchain obviates the necessity for maintaining numerous versions of identical documents (Delloitte, 2017).

Future of Blockchain in Finance and Banking

The prospective trajectory of blockchain technology within the realms of finance and banking is discussed. The utilisation of blockchain technology in the financial services industry is still in its early stages. The progressive advancement of BCT, which currently exhibits immaturity, is expected to undergo gradual refinement in the future. In the foreseeable future, it is anticipated that there will be two notable advancements in the field, namely interoperability and enhancements in transaction processing. These enhancements will enhance the utility of the technology for financial institutions.

The implementation of blockchain technology has the potential to significantly streamline the loan process. An illustration of the potential application of blockchain technology in the lending industry involves the utilisation of blockchain assets as collateral, circumventing the limitations associated with traditional credit scoring systems. The utilisation of blockchain technology has the potential to enhance peer-to-peer lending owing to its inherent security features. Efficient and secure peer-to-peer lending has the potential to bypass the rigorous criteria imposed by traditional financial institutions. The adoption of blockchain technology within the banking industry remains limited, while there is a gradual progression towards its wider implementation. Financial institutions, such as banks, must consider numerous streamlining processes while implementing blockchain technology. Firstly, it is imperative that financial institutions possess the necessary infrastructure to support blockchain technology and adhere to global norms in its implementation. The global implementation of blockchain can only be achieved under specific circumstances. The adoption of blockchain as a global standard offers notable benefits, including enhanced transparency in banking systems, expedited transaction processing, and decreased processing expenses. Overall, the prospects for blockchain technology in the financial sector appear quite promising.

Implications

In light of the increasing impact of blockchain-based technologies on the banking business, this chapter aims to explore the application of blockchain in the finance and banking sector. The imperative for the financial services sector to engage in innovation and explore novel technologies in order to enhance their offerings and operations is of utmost importance. If the current market leaders fail to adapt their products and engage in innovative practises, they will face disruption from emerging players, as seen by the emergence of numerous blockchain FinTech startups that are revolutionising financial management processes. Blockchain technology, as well as other distributed ledger platforms, provides numerous advantages for banking firms. It is imperative to acknowledge that financial companies must undergo a transformative shift in order to capitalise on the potential advantages offered by distributed and decentralised technologies and technology (Mark, 2023). It is imperative for financial institution managers to prioritise collaboration with the ecosystem prior to initiating any use cases. The implementation process required to gain acceptance of the new system within the ecosystem would entail a substantial operational endeavour, perhaps posing challenges to its overall adoption. Therefore, it is imperative for financial institution managers to exert considerable effort in persuading the ecosystem to choose a decentralised solution. The true advantages of blockchain technology would manifest when financial institutions collaborate with other participants within the ecosystem to reinvent their business models. Financial institution managers should prioritise the exploration of complex use cases, commonly referred to as "wicked problems," which are currently challenging to address. Conversely, they should allocate less attention to simple use cases, reserving them for later stages of internal maturity when comfort and familiarity have been established. The implementation of blockchain technology may incur significant expenses for addressing issues that either do not exist or might be resolved efficiently using pre-existing solutions. Financial institution managers are advised to embrace a mindset of disruption when considering the implementation of blockchain technology. This entails prioritising the development of innovative business models that prioritise the needs and preferences of customers. In order to facilitate the effective implementation of blockchain technology (BCT) and enhance the operational efficiency of the financial sharing centre, it is imperative to establish a robust system within the company that ensures the authenticity and validity of financial information. By leveraging the advantages of BCT and Fintech, it is essential to initiate the development of an application system that is exclusive to the company. This system will enable self-management and self-monitoring, thereby ensuring the seamless integration of BCT and driving substantial enhancements in the financial sharing centre. In the future, banks may want to establish digital currency as the prevailing form of currency.

CONCLUSION

The primary objective of this chapter was to examine the effects of blockchain technology on the banking industry. The literature review conducted in this study reveals that the impact of blockchain technology on the banking sector is anticipated to be substantial in various areas, including settlement and payment processes, traceability of transactions, expedited transaction speeds, cost reduction measures, capital market operations, and regulatory frameworks. The future economic system is expected to undergo significant transformation due to various innovations such as bitcoins, cryptocurrencies, artificial intelligence, and robotic solutions. Blockchain technology has gained significant prominence and has become a widely discussed topic among individuals across several domains. This technology has emerged as a result of the development of bitcoin and cryptocurrency. The technology in question is a distributed and collaborative ledger, wherein transactions may be conducted solely among participants without the need for a central governing body. This innovation has the potential to revolutionise financial services in the banking sector. This technology has the potential to reduce costs, mitigate fraudulent activities, and enhance transparency inside the financial system, particularly in the banking sector. Furthermore, this technology provides significant benefits to banks in terms of cross-border remittance, since it enables transactions to be completed within a matter of seconds, which is far faster than the existing system. In the future, it is quite likely that blockchain technology will become ubiquitous. However, the adoption of this technology will require a significant amount of time. Once fully integrated, blockchain has the potential to revolutionise genuine transactions, particularly in democratic societies where corruption is prevalent. Despite the occurrence seen in the preceding section. In order to remain abreast of advancements, it is imperative to have a repertoire of contemporary information, practical experience, and technological competencies. A transformation must occur, when all aspects of society undergo significant shifts due to technological advancements. The implementation of blockchain technology (BCT) is expected to require a significant amount of time in order to effectively address the disruptive factors that hinder the transformation of the Indian banking sector. The primary objective of this implementation is to enhance the speed, security, safety, transparency, and cost-effectiveness of transactions within the sector. It is vital for individuals to acquire knowledge pertaining to the subject matter, and it is highly recommended that efforts be made to promote its practical application. In conclusion, it is evident that blockchain technology possesses significant potential for revolutionising the banking system. Given the considerable potential of blockchain technology in the financial services sector, it is imperative for both industry stakeholders and governmental authorities to collaborate in order to promote the wider adoption of this technology. This collaboration should prioritise the implementation of appropriate safety measures and rigorous consumer safeguards. The historical adoption of a cautious and observant stance towards blockchain technology may be attributed to its initial novelty. However, the current state of blockchain technology has reached a level of maturity that necessitates prompt action. As various nations actively encourage and advance the implementation of blockchain applications, particularly within the financial services sector, it is imperative for private entities in numerous countries to further investigate the advantages of blockchain technology and apply it to tangible market-based solutions. These entities should be granted the opportunity to do so within a well-defined regulatory framework that does not hinder the progress of this emerging technology.

REFERENCES

Collomb, A., Sok, K. (2016). Blockchain/Distributed Ledger Technology (DLT): What Impact on the Financial Sector? *DigiWorld Economic Journal, 3*(103), 93-110.

Delloitte (2017). Blockchain in banking: While the interest is huge, challenges remain for large scale adoption. Available from: https://www2.deloitte.com/content/dam/Deloitte/in/Documents/strategy/in-strategy-innovation-blockchain-in-banking-noexp.pdf.

IBM (2023). Benefits of blockchain. Available from: https://www.ibm.com/blockchain/industries/financial-services.

Brown, C. (2020). More than a third of the world's largest banks use Ripple. Available from: https://www.crypto-news-flash.com/mehr-als-ein-drittel-der-groessten-banken-der-weltnutzen-ripple/ (Accessed on July 5, 2020.).

Casey, M., Crane, J., Gensler, G., Johnson, S., Narula, N. (2019). *The Impact of Blockchain Technology on*

Finance: A Catalyst for Change.. London: Centre for Economic Policy Research.

Dhanda, N. (2022). *Cryptocurrency and Blockchain: The future of Global Banking System..* IN: Regulatory Aspects of Artificial Intelligence on Blockchain.
[http://dx.doi.org/10.4018/978-1-7998-7927-5.ch009]

Ganatra, M. (2022). The use of blockchain in financial services. Available from: https://timesofindia.indiatimes.com/blogs/voices/the-use-of-blockchain-in-financial-services/.

Garcia, A. (2018b). IBM's blockchain app store wants to help banks cut costs. Available from: https://money.cnn.com/2018/07/30/technology/ibm-blockchain-app-store/ index.html.

Gupta, A. & Gupta, S. 2018. Blockchain technology: Application in Indian banking sector. *Delhi Business Review19*(2), 75-84. Available from: https://search.proquest.com/docview/2247499893?accountid=10007.

Gupta, M. (2018). *Blockchain for dummies.* (3rd ed.). Hoboken, NJ: John Wiley & Sons.

Harris, W.L., Wonglimpiyarat, J. (2019). Blockchain platform and future bank competition. *Foresight, 21*(6), 625-639.
[http://dx.doi.org/10.1108/FS-12-2018-0113]

Hillsberg, A. (2018). Can Blockchain Technology Impact Banking? We Analyse this Important Trend. Available from: https://www.comparethecloud.net/articles/ can-blockchain-technology-impact-banki-g-we-analyse-this-important-trend/ (Accessed: 30.07.2018).

Ho, F. (2016). What Blockchain Actually Means For The Future Of Banking. Available from: https://decentralize.today/what-blockchain-actually-means-for-the-future-of-banking-4dd868d020cf [Accessed: 30.07.2018].

Mark, V. R. (2023). Blockchain – 7 Benefits for the Financial Services Industry. Available from: https://londonspeakerbureau.com/blockchain-7-benefits-financial-industry/.

Petrov, D. (2019). The impact of blockchain and distributed ledger technology on financial services. *International Scientific Journal "Industry 4.0", 2*.

Portilla, D.L., Kappos, D.J., Ngo, M.V., Rosenthal-Larrea, S., Buretta J.D., & Fargo, C.K. (2022). Blockchain in the Banking Sector: A Review of the Landscape and Opportunities.

Pratt, M. K. (2023). 10 blockchain uses cases in finance that show value. Available from: https://www.techtarget.com/searchcio/feature/5-blockchain-use-cases-in-finance-that-show-value.

Sharma, J. (2022). Top 8 Ways Banks Benefit From Blockchain Tech. Available from: https://www.fintechweekly.com/magazine/articles/Top-8-Ways-Banks-Benefit-From-Blockchain-Technology .

Storm2 (2023). Benefits of Blockchain in Financial Services. Available from: https://storm2.com/ resources/type/storm2-voice/benefits-blockchain-financial-services/#:~:text=It%20also%20helps%20to%20 increase,in%20their%20products%20and%20services.

Ulatus (2022). The Future of Blockchain In Finance and Banking. Available from: https://www.ulatus.com/translation-blog/the-future-of-blockchain-in-finance-and-banking/.

Yomboi, J., Nangpiire, C., Kutochigaga, E.A., Majeed, M. (2021). The impact of the collapsed banks on customers in Ghana. *Asian Journal of Economics. Asian Journal of Economics, Business and Accounting, 21*(17), 15-25.
[http://dx.doi.org/10.9734/ajeba/2021/v21i1730487]

Zhang, Y., Zhang, C. (2022). Improving the Application of Blockchain Technology for Financial Security in Supply Chain Integrated Business Intelligence. *Secur. Commun. Netw., 2022*, 1-8.
[http://dx.doi.org/10.1155/2022/4980893]

CHAPTER 6

Big Data in Finance and Banking Sector

Mohammad Irfan[1,*], **Mohammed Majeed**[2], **Jonas Yomboi**[3], **Abdul-Razak Abubakari**[4] and **Evans Kelvin Gyau**[5]

[1] *NSB Academy, Business School, Bengaluru, Karnataka 560099, India*

[2] *Marketing Department, Tamale Technical University, Tamale, Ghana*

[3] *Accountancy Department, Valley View University, Oyibi-Ghana*

[4] *Entrepreneurship and Enterprise Development, Tamale Technical University, Tamale, Ghana*

[5] *Accountancy Department, Sunyani Technical University, Sunyani, Ghana*

Abstract: The rapid advancement of digital technology and the widespread adoption of global communication networks have led to significant transformations in the responsibilities of enterprises, the characteristics of value generation, and even economic structures. The main objective of this chapter is to discern prevailing trends in the utilisation of big data (BD) within the banking sector. This technology possesses the potential to effectively address future crises and expedite the identification of forthcoming opportunities. The advantages encompassed in this context encompass cost-effectiveness, customer experience, and customer pleasure, among others. Conversely, the obstacles faced encompass the management of large volumes of data and the prevention of fraudulent activities, among other issues. In the realm of banking and financial services, big data serves as a multifaceted solution, a strategic instrument, and a process-driven approach to digital transformation.

Keywords: Banking, Big data, Customer, Financial services, Security, Technology.

INTRODUCTION

With the advent of technological advances and the rapid growth and globalisation of pervasive communication networks, business functions, the characteristics of value generation, and even economic structures are undergoing significant transformations (Schwab, 2017). Part of the manual labour previously performed by humans was automated by mechanisation in the latter part of the nineteenth and late twentieth centuries, and with the advancement of information technology

---

* **Corresponding author Mohammad Irfan:** NSB Academy, Business School, Bengaluru, Karnataka 560099, India; E-mail: mohammad.irfan@aurouniversity.edu.in

Abdul-Razak Abubakari, Mohammed Majeed, Nurideen Alhassan and Jonas Yomboi (Eds.)

from the mid to late twentieth century, normal data analysis previously performed by humans was automated (Korinek & Stiglitz, 2017). Mustafa and Rahman(2015) found that the more widespread the use of IT and automation, the more benefits they would offer. Big data, AI, blockchain, and the Internet of Things are just a few of the new technologies ushering in the Fourth Industrial Revolution, which is reshaping our economy and way of life. More and more businesses these days have access to cutting-edge technology like this. The term "FinTech," a portmanteau of "finance" and "technology," describes the impact of technological advancements on the financial sector (McAuley, 2015). In the early 2000s, as e-commerce expanded to include more straightforward payment methods, the first examples of fintech emerged. Since most corporations at the time concentrated their efforts on improving their IT infrastructure, FinTech had less of an impact on the banking sector. However, the most recent trend demonstrates numerous applications in credit analysis, loan administration, and asset management utilising blockchain, AI, and IoT, separating its uses from the more conventional technology in FinTech (Bae, 2018). FinTech (Financial Technology) relies heavily on big data. To improve traditional banking services, FinTech implements cutting-edge technological solutions. In order to collect, analyse, and use huge and complicated datasets, big data plays a crucial role in FinTech (Vaidya, 2023). It aids FinTech firms in optimising financial procedures through data-driven decisions, risk assessment model development, and the provision of individualised services. Hence, the main objective of this chapter is to discern prevailing trends in the utilisation of big data (BD) within the banking sector.

Contribution

The objective of this study is to examine the present state of big data implementation within the financial services sector. This chapter specifically focuses on the impact of big data on the banking industry and the management of financial services. This study additionally highlights the advantages that contribute to the understanding of how big data impacts the field of finance. Additionally, certain obstacles have been presented. This study makes several contributions to the existing literature. This chapter will serve as a valuable addition to the existing body of literature, providing a foundation for future scholarly endeavours. This report provides an analysis of the advantages and obstacles encountered by managers while utilising big data in the context of banking services. The findings of this chapter make a valuable contribution to the current body of literature. This contribution will be beneficial to readers and researchers who are engaged in studying this topic. As a result of this study, all readers will gain a comprehensive understanding of the role of big data in the field of finance. Moreover, this study holds significance for scholars engaged in investigating this subject matter. This paper delves into the topic of big data, examining it from many financial viewpoints in order to enhance readers' comprehension. Hence, a significant endeavour has been undertaken to prioritise the examination of big data finance operations, specifically by assessing their multifaceted impact on the banking sector. The primary objective of this chapter is to discern present and prospective trends in the utilisation of artificial intelligence (AI) within the financial sector, employing methodologies rooted in big data analysis. This tool has the potential to effectively address future crises and anticipate prospective opportunities.

LITERATURE REVIEW

Big Data

"Big Data" refers to a comprehensive assemblage of data that is systematically organised, comprising elements of both structured and unstructured nature. This data holds the potential to be extracted for valuable insights and can be effectively utilised in many sophisticated analytical endeavours such as machine learning, predictive modelling, and other advanced analytics projects. Ostapchenya (2021) defines "big data" as a continuously expanding collection of structured and unstructured data in diverse formats that share a common context. According to Svitla (2023), the integration of big data analysis and storage networks, together with innovations that support big data analytics, has become a commonplace element within data management frameworks in various corporate contexts. The primary characteristics of this technology encompass volume, velocity, diversity, value, and authenticity. The magnitude of data sets obtained from diverse sources exceeds the capacity of our conventional information processing technologies. The significance of big data in the context of intelligent decision-making cannot be overlooked (Abkenar, Kashani, Mahdipour, & Jameii, 2021). The need to conduct thorough analysis and research in decision-making is widely acknowledged in the digital age (Ain *et al.*, 2019; Mohammed *et al.*, 2024). The significance of big data is increasing steadily, capturing the interest of both academics and scholars (Salehan & Kim, 2016). The concept of "big data" has emerged as a means to augment the collection of data from diverse sources like employees, consumers, suppliers, and other relevant parties (Wolfert, Ge, Verdouw, & Bogaardt, 2017). The topic is garnering attention, particularly due to the passage of time and developments in technology (Liu, Soroka, Han, Jian, & Tang, 2020). The prevalence of this phenomenon in numerous organisations has led senior management to express a willingness to allocate resources towards big data initiatives (Dubey & Gunasekaran, 2015).

In 2019, the Financial Stability Board released a study emphasising the importance of diligent surveillance on the utilisation of Big Data tools by companies (Ostapchenya, 2021). The aforementioned prominent entities, including Microsoft, Amazon, eBay, Baidu, Apple, Facebook, and Tencent, possess extensive datasets that undoubtedly confer upon them a distinct advantage in the competitive landscape. Furthermore, alongside their primary business activities, several corporations have already incorporated financial services into their repertoire, including asset management, payments, and lending activities, for the benefit of their clients.

Big Data in Finance and Banking

The field of finance is significantly influenced and shaped by the utilisation of large-scale data, sometimes referred to as "big data." This comprises the extensive impact and influence that data has on various aspects of finance, including financial goods and services. According to Vaidya (2023), the field of study referred to as "financial analytics" covers a diverse array of data pertaining to various aspects of the financial industry, including but not limited to the banking and finance industries markets, organisations, managerial practises, financing, evaluation of risks, and fraud detection. According to Alsmadi *et al.* (2019, 2022), the advent of the age of technology has brought about substantial changes and transformations in several aspects of life and cognition, mostly due to the emergence of big data. Presently, investors, whether they are businesses or individuals, make judgements by relying on statistical patterns and projection methodologies (Wamba, *et al.*, 2017). When engaging in investments within the financial sector, individuals and businesses alike make decisions based on many forms of analysis (Akter, Wamba, Gunasekaran, Dubey, & Childe, 2016). Similarly, the corporate sector uses this strategy to enhance performance by efficiently managing existing money and working capital (Asad, 2011). The banking sector, which holds a significant influence in the financial industry, has been allocating substantial resources towards the implementation of big data analytics (Power, Heavin, McDermott, & Daly, 2018). The banking industry produces vast amounts of data, encompassing customer information, financial product details, transaction records, and more. The data is utilised to help decision-making systems by integrating it with external data derived from social media or marketing websites (Saleem *et al.*, 2020). The utilisation of large-scale data sets, sometimes referred to as "big data," within the domains of finance and banking. The term "big data" encompasses vast quantities of structured and unstructured data, sometimes measured in petabytes, that can be leveraged by banks and financial institutions for the purpose of forecasting customer behaviour and formulating strategic approaches. The financial industry generates a substantial volume of data. Structured data refers to information that is managed and utilised within an organisation to facilitate the generation of vital insights for decision-making purposes (Majeed, 2022). The volume of unstructured data is growing exponentially as it is collected from many channels, presenting significant prospects for analysis (Svitla, 2023). The banking and financial services sector produces a substantial amount of data, totaling more than 2.5 quintillion bytes. According to Vinjamuri (2021), the banking business may leverage the data-backed digital footprints generated by each activity inside the industry, hence creating several potentials for capitalization. In contemporary times, a significant number of banks employ big data as a means to acquire a competitive edge, a practice seen as pertinent to their operational endeavours (Assis *et al.*, 2019). The utilisation of big data analytics is seeing a persistent upward trajectory due to its imperative nature for survival in the current era of intense competition (George, Martine, & Pentland, 2014). The financial sector presently employs applications encompassing social media, websites, risk management, security intelligence, and fraud detection or assessment (Liu, 2015). The advent of technology has enabled banks to effectively utilise data in order to make informed and strategic decisions. In recent years, there has been a growing trend in the banking industry towards the use of big data analytics. This trend is driven by the digitization of operational processes inside banks, which necessitates the utilisation of various technologies such as Hadoop and RDBMS for the purpose of analysing data and achieving business benefits.

On a daily basis, an immense amount of capital flows through international financial markets, necessitating analysts to diligently monitor this data with the utmost accuracy, safeguarding measures, and expeditiousness in order to formulate projections, identify trends, and devise anticipatory strategies. The value of data is contingent upon the methodologies employed for its collection, processing, storage, and analysis. There is a growing trend among analysts to choose cloud-based data solutions due to the limitations of legacy systems in handling unstructured and segregated data without requiring complex and extensive IT involvement (Svitla, 2023). Banks that leverage big data have the capacity to make well-informed assessments in areas such as enhancing customer care, preventing fraudulent activities, optimising client targeting, evaluating the effectiveness of different channels, and assessing levels of risk exposure. This is made possible by their ability to analyse diverse forms of data.

Financial institutions, being non-digital natives, have undergone a protracted conversion process, including significant alterations in both behaviour and technology. In recent years, the banking industry pertaining to big data has witnessed significant technical progress, enabling the provision of convenient, customised, and secure solutions for businesses. Consequently, the utilisation of big data analytics in the banking sector has brought about a significant transformation, impacting not just the internal processes of individual businesses but also the overall landscape of the financial services industry. This analysis will examine some tangible ways in which the utilisation of big data has facilitated the modernization and transformation of the finance industry.

Benefits of Big Data in Finance and Banking

The Practice of Categorizing Buyers

The utilisation of big data in the banking sector enables banking institutions to create customer profiles, enabling them to provide personalised services to individual clients by using their banking history and transactional patterns accumulated throughout their tenure with the bank (Svitla, 2023). This capability empowers them to develop customised strategies and remedies for their clientele. This enhances the consumer experience and aids banks in distinguishing themselves and maintaining customer loyalty. Banks have the ability to strategically tailor various products to certain consumer segments, taking into consideration their demographic characteristics.

The Determination of Lending Policies

Lending constitutes a significant decision within the realm of the banking sector. Selecting the appropriate consumer who possesses both creditworthiness and financial stability is of utmost importance in order to effectively settle outstanding debts. Furthermore, in the past, financial institutions have traditionally depended on credit rating organisations to evaluate the creditworthiness of their clients. However, this approach has been criticised for its limited perspective, as it only takes into account certain factors while disregarding others (Mathur, 2022). By leveraging the utilisation of big data analytics, financial institutions are able to incorporate more variables, such as consumer expenditure patterns, transaction characteristics, and related aspects, into their loan evaluation processes. The availability of additional data and expertise has expanded the scope of opportunities for bankers and financial institutions.

The Adherence to Regulatory Requirements

The utilisation of big data analytics and business intelligence (BI) tools significantly enhances the efficacy and efficiency of record-keeping and regulatory compliance. According to Mathur (2022), organisations have the ability to efficiently oversee and monitor a wide range of regulatory processes, including tax obligations and record-keeping requirements mandated by central banks. The management of compliance in legacy systems was a laborious and time-consuming process. However, the utilisation of business intelligence (BI) tools has significantly simplified this task. These tools consolidate information in a concise manner, enabling decision-makers to easily adhere to compliance in a manner that was previously unattainable. Moreover, when appropriately programmed, these systems have the capability to effectively handle such regulatory requirements, hence mitigating the potential for errors and fraudulent activities resulting from human involvement.

Cybersecurity

The field of cybersecurity encompasses the protection of computer systems, networks, and data from unauthorised access. The prevalence of cyberattacks and online financial crime is widespread, and embezzlement is a significant challenge even for highly reputable organisations globally. Numerous prominent institutions, notably financial institutions, have experienced instances of cyberattacks resulting in the compromise of both financial assets and client data. Banks have the capacity to establish resilient internal control systems by leveraging big data and AI technologies. This is due to the fact that these tasks can potentially be executed by individuals within the organisation, while also enabling the monitoring of consumer behaviour through the use of advanced algorithms. Furthermore, in the context of financial terrorism, organisations have the potential to engage in proactive collaboration and knowledge sharing with governmental agencies by leveraging their business intelligence and big data analytics capabilities. This collaboration aims to effectively address and minimise the associated risks.

The Identification and Prevention of Fraudulent Activities

One of the foremost formidable issues confronting the banking sector in contemporary times pertains to the identification and prevention of fraudulent activities and dubious transactions. The banking industry is currently facing a huge challenge in the rapidly developing digital landscape, namely the increasing occurrence of cyberattacks that have revealed the susceptibility of critical consumer data. By doing an analysis of user behaviour and expenditure patterns, financial institutions have been able to promptly detect instances of fraud and scams (Vaidya, 2023). This capability is facilitated by the utilisation of machine learning techniques and the analysis of data. Financial institutions possess the capability to proactively identify instances of fraudulent activity by employing data analysis techniques and leveraging statistical computing methodologies. According to Mathur (2022), the utilisation of distinctive fraud detection algorithms, which monitor and analyse spending habits and other behavioural patterns, enables the identification and assessment of individuals who may be at risk of experiencing severe financial distress and consequently be tempted to engage in fraudulent activities against banking institutions. Retail banks, investment banks, private equity firms, and other financial institutions have specialised risk management departments that extensively utilise big data and business analytics. The utilisation of big data in the banking sector facilitates the establishment of measures to prevent unauthorised transactions (Mathur, 2022). Additionally, it will guarantee the comprehensive safety and security of the banking sector. Moreover, financial institutions have the capability to leverage big data in order to proactively combat fraudulent activities and enhance client confidence. This may be achieved by the continuous monitoring of customer spending patterns and the detection of any anomalous behaviour.

The Utilisation of Intelligence Tools

Machine learning plays a significant role in enhancing fraud detection and prevention efforts, mostly driven by the utilisation of extensive datasets. The application of analytics in analysing purchasing trends has resulted in a reduction in credit card security threats. In instances where highly secure and valuable credit card information is compromised, banks have developed the capability to promptly initiate a freeze on the affected card and transaction, while simultaneously notifying the cardholder of the potential security risks involved.

The Classification or Termination of Customers

The banking industry benefits from the implementation of big data, as it offers a highly advantageous and effective characteristic. The system possesses the capability to classify customers according to their financial behaviours, encompassing income generation, expenditure patterns, savings habits, and investment practices. The identification and categorization of customers' pertinent and consequential data are conducted in accordance with their financial needs (Svitla, 2023). This enabled bank management to gain a more comprehensive understanding of the financial service thresholds that required either upgrading or downgrading. This functionality has facilitated and continues to facilitate the strategic decision-making process of bank executives in relation to interest rates and other financial services.

The Enhancement of Operational Efficiency in Manual Procedures

Scalability is an inherent characteristic of data integration solutions, enabling them to expand in accordance with evolving business requirements. According to Svitla (2023), credit card companies have the potential to streamline their operations, decrease the number of IT personnel required, and get valuable insights into their customers' everyday behaviours by leveraging comprehensive daily transaction data.

Risk Management

Risk management is a strategic process that involves identifying, assessing, and mitigating potential risks in order to minimise their negative impact on firms. The utilisation of big data analytics within the finance industry has the ability to enhance the decision-making process of financial enterprises by effectively spotting pertinent trends and potential risks (Svitla, 2023). The utilisation of data analysis has enabled the identification of potential dangers in real time, thereby providing a means to protect clients from fraudulent activities. Financial institutions have the capacity to facilitate this outcome by establishing robust risk management systems, a feat that may be accomplished by acquiring the requisite information. Furthermore, financial institutions employ data analytics techniques to improve prediction models for assessing loan risks and forecasting expected expenses (Vaidya, 2023). Furthermore, these institutions utilise the data in order to fulfil legal and regulatory obligations, mitigate operational risk, deter fraudulent activities, and address issues related to information asymmetry. The utilisation of machine learning is progressively being employed in significant financial decision-making processes, such as investments and loans. Decisions informed by predictive analytics encompass a comprehensive range of factors, including economic conditions, client segmentation, and business capital, in order to proactively anticipate potential risks such as flawed investments or payment issues. The effective management of risks, particularly operational risks, fraud risks, and credit risks, has posed a persistent issue for banks since their inception. This is the point at which the concept of "big data" becomes relevant. The utilisation of big data analytics is observed in several significant domains pertaining to the field of risk management. The utilisation of sophisticated big data analytics tools and techniques has the potential to significantly enhance the predictive capabilities of risk models, improve system response time, and provide broader risk coverage. The utilisation of big data analytics in the banking sector can provide significant assistance in ensuring compliance with legal and regulatory obligations, particularly in the areas of integrity risk and credit risk. The significance of big data analytics in the banking industry is substantial, particularly with regard to risk management.

Customised Banking Solutions

The integration of big data with efficient tools and technology enables banks to gain a more comprehensive understanding of individual clients through the analysis of received inputs (Mathur, 2022). This includes their patterns of investment, patterns of shopping, factors driving their investment decisions, and their individual or financial histories. One potential approach to mitigating churn is through the utilisation of comprehensive customer profiles and data, enabling the ability to forecast and proactively address client attritionThe banking business utilises big data for the purpose of gaining insights into its customer base. Consequently, organisations develop and deliver customised products, services, and other offers by leveraging pre-established client profiles to cater to their unique requirements (Shalimov, 2023).

Effective Analysis of Customer Feedback

In order to get valuable insights and make informed decisions, it is crucial for businesses to effectively analyse customer feedback. This process involves systematically examining and interpreting the information provided by customers. By means of feedback, big data tools have the capability to furnish banks with information regarding consumer inquiries, remarks, and apprehensions. The provision of feedback aids individuals in promptly formulating their responses (Mathur, 2022). Customer loyalty can be fostered by a company that demonstrates a commitment to valuing customer input and engaging in timely communication.

Enhanced Decision-Making

Through the examination of extensive datasets, financial institutions have the capacity to discern prevailing patterns and trends in consumer behaviour. This enables them to enhance their predictive capabilities, thereby optimising their operational strategies in alignment with anticipated future outcomes. The utilisation of big data analytics in the financial services sector offers the opportunity to access and analyse extensive volumes of data, thereby enabling the generation of more informed and knowledgeable decision-making processes. This facilitates the enhancement of risk management methods and product development strategies for organisations.

Enhanced Customer Experience

In contemporary times, there has been a notable shift in the dynamics of the interaction between banks and consumers, wherein people now engage in transient associations with several banks. According to Hussain and Prieto (2016), contemporary banks lack a comprehensive understanding of their customers' preferences, purchasing habits, and behaviours. Therefore, big data technologies play a central role in facilitating client-centricity within this emerging paradigm. The application of big data analytics in the financial services sector facilitates the acquisition of valuable information pertaining to client preferences and requirements. Consequently, financial service providers are empowered to deliver personalised experiences that are custom-tailored to the unique demands of individual users. By possessing this type of understanding, financial institutions have the ability to generate more pertinent proposals for their customers. The maintenance of satisfactory customer relations is facilitated through the collection and analysis of customer data, the provision of beneficial offers, and the assurance of transactional security (Vaidya, 2023). The advent of digital technology in the financial industry and the growing prevalence of customers engaging with brands or organisations through digital platforms present a potential avenue for financial services organisations to augment their customer engagement efforts and actively enhance the customer experience (Hussain & Prieto, 2016). There is a prevalent argument that financial institutions should prioritise the utilisation of big data technology in order to maintain a competitive edge or just remain on par with their rivals. In order to facilitate this objective, the utilisation of big data technology and analytical methodologies can be important in extracting valuable insights from emerging unstructured data sources, such as social media platforms.

Cost Optimisation

The process of cost optimisation involves identifying and implementing strategies to minimise expenses while maximising value and efficiency. According to the findings of Hasan, Popp, and Oláh (2020), the utilisation of big data and analytics in the financial services sector has been observed to contribute to a reduction in operational costs through the automation of manual processes, including but not limited to fraud detection and compliance checks. The implementation of this approach obviates the necessity for expensive human labour, while also guaranteeing precision and dependability in outcomes. Furthermore, it enables organisations to promptly identify potential concerns before they escalate into significant challenges, resulting in time and cost savings in the long term.

Enhancing Market Trading Analysis

The digitization of trading in the financial markets emerged several years ago in response to the increasing need for expedited trade execution. Trading techniques that utilise advanced algorithms for the purpose of swiftly engaging in financial market transactions are significantly advantageous due to the utilisation of big data. Market data can be seen as a form of big data in its own right. The phenomenon under consideration exhibits a substantial magnitude, emanates from many origins, and is characterised by an extraordinary pace of generation. Nevertheless, the abundance of big data does not automatically result in knowledge that can be effectively utilised (Hussain & Prieto, 2016). The true advantage of big data resides in the efficient extraction of actionable information and its seamless integration with other data sources. The integration of market data from various markets and locations, along with diverse asset classes, can facilitate the creation of richer hybrid datasets. These datasets are formed by combining structured and unstructured data from different sources. This offers a full and cohesive perspective on the current market condition, serving several purposes including signal generation, trade execution, profit and loss (P&L) analysis, and risk assessment, all in real time. As a result, it facilitates more efficient trading practices. The tremendous growth in demand for expeditious market trade execution has emerged as a significant catalyst for the integration of big data inside the banking industry. The emergence of big data analytics has provided financial organisations with the opportunity to achieve the desired levels of speed and accuracy. Furthermore, the advancements in big data analytics have enabled banks to utilise intricate algorithms for the purpose of swiftly engaging in financial market trading. The collection of data from many marketplaces can be inputted into sophisticated big data technologies in order to generate comprehensive, amalgamated data sets that can provide an up-to-date, all-encompassing perspective of the market situation. Therefore, financial institutions possess the capability to analyse prevailing market trends and afterwards make informed decisions that are in line with their organisational objectives.

Enhanced Security Measures

Big Data solutions offer enhanced security and compliance controls that safeguard both consumers' personal information and sensitive company assets against cyberattacks and unscrupulous actors. These instruments serve to facilitate adherence to regulatory requirements pertaining to finance or banking operations, thereby mitigating the legal risks associated with penalties or fines imposed by governmental entities for non-compliance.

Segmentation

Customer Segmentation

Customer segmentation is a process that involves dividing a customer base into distinct groups based on specific characteristics, behaviours, or preferences. This practice allows businesses to better understand their customers. The implementation of customer segmentation strategies enables banks to enhance their ability to effectively target their clientele through the utilisation of tailored marketing campaigns. According to Mathur (2022), subsequent ads are customised to effectively address the specific requirements of the target audience. By integrating machine learning and artificial intelligence with big data, financial institutions will gain significant knowledge regarding user behaviour. Additionally, it enables organisations to optimise their customer experience based on the findings of Mathur (2022). Moreover, banks will possess the capability to classify their clientele according to diverse criteria, such as favoured credit card expenditures or overall financial assets, through the ability to monitor and record each consumer activity.

The utilisation of big data in the banking industry has the potential to facilitate customer segmentation by categorising clients according to their financial actions. According to Shalimov (2023), this framework has the potential to serve as a basis for examining client behaviour, implementing more impactful marketing efforts, and identifying the optimal strategy for engaging various target segments. Following the preliminary examination of the income-expenditure framework, the bank categorises its clientele into various segments based on specific factors (Ostapchenya, 2021). This information facilitates the provision of appropriate services to clients in subsequent instances. Consequently, the workers of the financial institution are able to enhance their sales of supplementary goods and effectively engage consumers with personalised offers. Furthermore, the financial institution has the capability to assess the anticipated expenses and revenues of its clientele for the upcoming month, thereby formulating comprehensive strategies to guarantee a positive net profit and optimise earnings.

Challenges of Big Data in Finance and Banking

It is important to take into account the restrictions that arise while utilising big data in the fields of finance and banking. The subsequent are specific concerns that are frequently associated with the phenomenon of big data.

The Lack of Compatibility Between Culture and Infrastructure

Vaidya (2023) asserts that a considerable proportion of banks still rely on antiquated and rigid information technology infrastructures, encompassing data operations and numerous legacy systems. The integration of big data is frequently regarded as a minor ancillary action and is hindered by cultural influences. Numerous financial institutions abstain from undertaking data initiatives as a result of their limited understanding of the potential advantages of data analytics in augmenting their fundamental business operations.

Insufficient Proficiency

Several organisations demonstrate a comprehension of the data and its inherent possibilities. Nevertheless, the organisation is deficient in the requisite human capital and skills to adequately address the discrepancy that exists between the accessible data and the possible opportunities.

Difficulties Faced by Legacy Systems in Keeping up with the Rapid Pace of Technological Changes

The considerable prevalence of fintech adoption is unsurprising. Mathur (2022) argues that traditional financial institutions have a disadvantage in comparison to customer-centric and nimble startups. Nevertheless, the difficulties become significantly more evident in the realm of big data, given that a substantial portion of current systems lack the necessary capabilities to efficiently handle the escalating magnitude of data. The employment of an outdated infrastructure for the purpose of collecting, storing, and analysing the required volumes of data has the potential to undermine the overall stability of the system. As a result, firms are required to enhance their processing capacity or undergo a thorough system redesign in order to efficiently tackle the situation.

Complexity

The notion of "intricacy" pertains to the degree of intricacy or challenge inherent in a given system or problem. The intricacy of the data presents a significant obstacle. Several key issues arise in this particular setting, including scalability, noise, storage constraints, and measurement imperfections. Errors and problems can develop during data collection procedures that are conducted with specific aims in mind. In order to safeguard crucial information, it is crucial to furnish clear and precise guidelines regarding the implementation of filters (Vaidya, 2023). The generation of a substantial quantity of data from various sources is a widespread occurrence, and the lack of data is a notable cause for concern. Furthermore, the factors pertaining to the quality and dependability of data carry significant significance within this particular context.

Insights into Client Behaviour and Trends

Data technologies and analytical tools provide financial services firms with a significant opportunity to gain in-depth insights into client behaviour and trends. Nevertheless, organisations still encounter difficulties when it comes to executing concrete actions in response to this data (Vaidya, 2023). The failure to effectively utilise acquired resources and expertise creates a squandered opportunity for a firm to produce income.

Risk of Large Data

As the volume of data expands, the corresponding amount of risk also escalates. Moreover, it is crucial to recognise that the existence of data inherently carries a degree of danger, especially considering the aforementioned historical problem (Mathur, 2022). Ensuring the security of user data is of utmost importance for banking institutions, necessitating a consistent prioritisation of this matter. Furthermore, there is a growing level of stringency in regulations pertaining to data security.

The Safeguarding of Data and the Preservation of Privacy

The absence of a precise and universally accepted definition of regulation in several countries poses a substantial barrier to the prompt and comprehensive adoption of regulatory measures. The present condition pertaining to the ownership and utilisation of customer data within the industry is marked by a dearth of clarity, rendering it challenging to ascertain the legal permissibility of certain actions. Vaidya (2023) highlights notable concerns with privacy and security.

The Administration of Large-scale Data

The administration of large-scale data poses further challenges. The management of data poses significant challenges for businesses due to the extensive range of data types and their overall volume. This effect becomes increasingly apparent when individuals attempt to differentiate between important knowledge and irrelevant content. The frequency of important data is increasing; nonetheless, a significant amount of irrelevant data continues to exist, hence requiring careful categorization (Mathur, 2022). This suggests that organisations must improve their methods for assessing larger amounts of data and, if possible, discover new uses for data that were previously deemed insignificant (Mihet & Philippon, 2019). Despite the aforementioned challenges, the benefits of employing big data in the banking industry definitely outweigh any potential risks. The significance of data lies in its capacity to generate significant insights, optimise the allocation of resources, and result in cost reductions.

Future of Big Data in Finance and Banking

Currently, the utilisation of analytics in the field of finance remains rather broad. Nevertheless, the forthcoming iteration of analytics is poised to provide state-of-the-art insights within a narrower scope, focusing on particular industries. This phenomenon will signify the emergence of a banking landscape characterised by a heightened level of customization and the utilisation of many communication channels. This capability will encompass a range of data types, including geographic information system (GIS) data, business data, movement data, process data, and other relevant data sources. The field of finance analytics is expected to make significant advancements, enabling the provision of accurate insights as well as goods for many industries such as online shopping, production, process administration, and educational solutions, among others. The field of forecasting and analytics is in its nascent stages, but as it continues to develop, there will likely be a proliferation of specialised analytics techniques that will become commonplace. These techniques will be sufficiently robust to generate precise forecasts by leveraging the vast amounts of data available through big data analytics. During this phase, a significant portion of the analytics procedures will be automated through the utilisation of machine learning and advanced artificial intelligence techniques. The level of competitiveness within the financial industry will increasingly hinge upon a company's readiness to adopt and effectively utilise technological tools in order to cater to its clientele. Regulatory bodies are progressively enhancing their comprehension of big data and strengthening their efforts to ensure responsible utilisation of said data. Firms that fail to prioritise data security will face significant repercussions. These repercussions will be imposed by governmental entities in the form of monetary fines and penalties, as well as by customers through the erosion of confidence. The task at hand is increasingly challenging due to the advent of the Internet of Things. Financial institutions that prioritise this matter will see significant success. Emerging technologies necessitate novel skill sets and industry standards. It is plausible that in the foreseeable future, novel vocations in predictive analytics and product analytics will arise, wherein proficient individuals will harness the potential of big data to forecast future trends and provide recommendations for product development. Data science specialists may choose to specialise in several sectors, including but not limited to business expertise, consumer technology, and manufacturing. Financial institutions cater to a wide range of customers with varying needs and patterns of behaviour. The implementation of customer segmentation strategies will facilitate the transition of the bank from a broad-based organisation to one that categorises its clients into distinct groups and tailors its marketing efforts accordingly. Currently, big data is being utilised by institutions to analyse client behaviour and trends in expenditure. In forthcoming times, the process of client segmentation is expected to progress significantly, incorporating specialised items supported by big data (BD) analysis. With the increasing operationalization and sophistication of deep learning and big data, it is anticipated that the sector will embark on new trajectories diverging from the prevailing patterns. The implementation of AI-only financial applications could potentially represent one of the aforementioned transformations. Additionally, it may include abandoning the user interface (UI) that individuals have become accustomed to in favour of a more streamlined, user-friendly, and adaptable interface facilitated by automated programmes (bots) that provide a personalised experience tailored to each user.

Implications

This chapter has a multitude of implications. Frequently, inaccurate outcomes arise as a consequence of users' limited comprehension or their failure to grasp the model's comprehensibility (Tang, Luo, & Zhang, 2019). Occasionally, the accuracy of computations may be compromised as a result of the implementation of cleaning strategies, which might inadvertently remove crucial information and thus lead to the failure of the prediction model (Russell, 2018). Hence, it is recommended that during the process of data cleansing, meticulous attention be given to following well-defined procedures. One significant concern, as previously noted, pertains to the collection method or trimming process. It is crucial to ensure that this process accommodates the utilisation of suitable sensors, particularly when dealing with financial records. It is imperative that the inherent noise does not compromise the essential essence of the data (Yang, Chen, Shi, & Wen, 2018). It is important to address any inconsistencies and clearly identify assumptions in financial modelling to prevent consumers from obtaining misleading findings (Giebe, Hammerström, & Zwerenz, 2019). The inherent uncertainties, rapidity, diversity, and lack of confidence can be mitigated through the provision of more dependable outcomes. When consumers are in the process of acquiring results and making decisions, it is advisable for them to utilise artificial intelligence techniques instead of relying solely on conventional data handling platforms. In conclusion, it is appropriate to assert that, given the financial challenges associated with big data, there is a need for additional scholarly investigation in this domain. This research ought to prioritise the development of even more robust models. The development of models should prioritise minimising assumptions and ensuring their applicability remains flexible in accordance with situational analysis. Specifically, in the context of financial markets, the management of money, and financial decision-making, the effective utilisation of these models can lead to competitiveness. There is a necessity to establish linkages between financial elements and big data. The notion of "big data" has recently emerged in the finance industry, therefore creating a substantial demand for research in financial risk management and the modelling of financial instruments. Therefore, the present study posits that research pertaining to big data ought to adhere to the same academic criteria as other publications in the field of finance.

CONCLUSION

The main objective of this chapter is to discern prevailing trends in the utilisation of big data in the financial sector. This tool possesses the capability to effectively address future crises and expedite the identification of future opportunities. In order to anticipate forthcoming opportunities resulting from recent changes, an examination was conducted on emerging trends within the domains of finance and business development, which have recently gained prominence within the financial industry. The primary focus of this chapter pertains to the many challenges and advantages associated with big data (BD). The field of finance is significantly influenced by the utilisation of large volumes of data, sometimes referred to as "big data." This comprises the extensive impact and influence that data has on various aspects of finance, including financial goods and services. The subject matter comprises a diverse array of data that encompasses all aspects of the financial industry, including sectors, markets, institutions, management practices, credit services, risk analysis, and fraud detection. Financial institutions have already been utilising big data for the purpose of analysing market trends and client behaviour. However, there remains a significant amount of work that needs to be undertaken in this area. An examination of this nature is highly necessary from the perspectives of customers, businesses, and compliance. The utilisation of Big Data within the banking sector is experiencing significant advancements. Through the integration of big data, financial institutions can enhance their service offerings in a timely fashion and concurrently mitigate operating expenditures. The implementation of big data practises enables individuals to recognise the advantages associated with big data.

REFERENCES

Hariri, R.H., Fredericks, E.M., Bowers, K.M. (2019). Uncertainty in big data analytics: survey, opportunities, and challenges. *J. Big Data, 6*(1), 44.
[http://dx.doi.org/10.1186/s40537-019-0206-3]

Hasan, M.M., Popp, J., Oláh, J. (2020). Current landscape and influence of big data on finance. *J. Big Data, 7*(1), 21.
[http://dx.doi.org/10.1186/s40537-020-00291-z]

Hussain, K., & Prieto, E. (2006). Big data in the finance and insurance sectors. In J. M. Cavanillas, E. Curry, & W. Wahlster (Eds.), *New horizons for a data-driven economy*, 3-12. Springer.
[http://dx.doi.org/10.1007/978-3-319-21569-3_12]

Mathur, V. (2022). Big Data In Banking Industry: Benefits, Uses and Challenges. Available from: https://www.analyticssteps.com/blogs/big-data-banking-industry-benefits-uses-and-challenges.

Majeed, M., Khalid, A.M., Yomboi, J., Nkayi, K. (2024). Challenges of SMEs Adoption of Big Data in Africa. *Informatics and Emerging Technologies, 3*, 30-39.
[http://dx.doi.org/10.2174/9789815223378124030006]

Ostapchenya, D. (2021). The Role of Big Data in Banking: How do Modern Banks Use Big Data? Available from: https://www.finextra.com/blogposting/20446/the-role-of-big-data-in-banking--how-do-modern-banks-use-big-data.

Svitla (2023). Big Data for Banking: Use Cases, Features, Toolkits, Skillset. Available from: https://svitla.com/blog/big-data-for-banking-use-cases-features-toolkits-skillset.

Shalimov, A. (2023). Big Data in the Banking Industry: The Main Challenges and Use Cases. Available from: https://easternpeak.com/blog/big-data-in-banking-and-financial-services/.

Vaidya, D. (2023). Big Data In Finance. Available from: https://www.wallstreetmojo.com/big-data--n-finance/#Applications.

Vinjamuri, S.R. (2021). The Challenges of Big Data in the Banking Industry. Available from: https://www.linkedin.com/pulse/challenges-big-data-banking-industry-sandeep-reddy-vinjamuri.

CHAPTER 7

Machine Learning Revolution Transforming Banking with Advanced Analytics

Victoria Manu[1,*]

[1] *Accountancy Department, Valley View University, Oyibi-Ghana*

Abstract: The banking sector has been revolutionised by the rise of machine learning (ML) applications. The banking industry generates a tremendous amount of data, and ML has emerged as a useful tool for analysing this data to increased efficiency, better serve customers, and better manage risks. As such, this chapter's focus is on ML's applications in the banking and financial industries. Large amounts of information related to transactions may be analysed in real-time with the help of ML methods in the finance and banking sectors, allowing for the detection of fraudulent actions, the prevention of monetary losses, and the protection of customers. In general, ML has the potential to revolutionise the banking industry by helping financial institutions better cater to their customers' individual needs, streamline their risk management processes, and deliver superior service.

Keywords: Banking, Finance, Fintech, Machine learning, Technology.

INTRODUCTION

Machine learning is becoming increasingly used in the banking sector. These days, you may utilise machine learning (ML) for anything from calculating risk to making trading judgements. It has altered business processes and information management in the banking sector. The banking industry produces a massive amount of data, including records of transactions, information on customers, and other forms of financial data. Machine learning algorithms can examine this information to look for trends and outliers and forecast future outcomes. Machine learning has found a lot of use in the banking industry, particularly in the area of fraud detection. Rapid detection of fraud is crucial to preventing losses in the banking business, where it is a pervasive problem. Transaction information can be analysed by machine learning algorithms for suspicious trends and outliers. Credit scoring is another major use of machine learning in banking. The financial sound-

---

[*] **Corresponding author Victoria Manu:** Accountancy Department, Valley View University, Oyibi-Ghana;
E-mail: victoria.manu@stu.edu.gh

Abdul-Razak Abubakari, Mohammed Majeed, Nurideen Alhassan and Jonas Yomboi (Eds.)

ness of potential customers is evaluated by banks using credit scores. A person's credit score can be calculated using a wide variety of characteristics, including credit history, job history, and algorithmic methods for machine learning (Aravind, 2023). As a result, financial institutions will be able to make more informed decisions regarding lending and mitigate default risk. The financial services industry is another that can employ machine learning to better serve its customers. With the help of machine learning algorithms, financial institutions can evaluate client data, including transaction and web surfing history to make tailored suggestions and offers. Machine learning is having an ever-increasing impact on commercial applications, with many solutions now in use and many more being researched. The detection, measurement, reporting, and management of risks inside financial institutions have come under increased scrutiny in the wake of the global financial crisis. Developments in banking and risk management, as well as existing and forthcoming digital solutions, have been the subject of extensive academic and professional investigation in recent years (Van Liebergen 2017; Deloitte University Press 2017; Oliver Wyman 2017). Concurrently, machine learning has become increasingly influential in corporate applications, with numerous solutions already in use and many more being considered. Not enough research appears to have been performed on the use of ML in the administration of market banks and financial services (Leo *et al*., 2019). There have been a lot of papers written about portfolio or investment risk management and its relation to market volatility or market risk. When looking at it through the lens of bank risk management, however, the literature seems thin (MetricStream, 2018). The goal of this chapter is to assess the current state of research on machine learning as it relates to banking and finance industry management, given its recent prominence as an emerging business enabler. The purpose of this review paper is to examine and evaluate the use of ML in banking management, to pinpoint management issues that have been understudied, and to offer direction for future research.

Contribution

The chapter offers many contributions, especially for future researchers who will venture into financial technology and specifically ML. The study also provided managers with the benefits of ML in the banking and financial sector so that they could quickly adopt it. Finally, we have provided the challenges for managers to be careful of. All these will lead to efficiency in the banking sector.

LITERATURE REVIEW

Machine Learning (ML)

Machine learning, sometimes known as ML, is a subfield within the discipline of computer engineering and the field of artificial intelligence (AI). The concept of machine learning (ML) was first coined by Arthur Samuel during his tenure at IBM in 1959. Samuel employed this word primarily to characterise the pattern recognition tasks that facilitated the "learning" aspect of the early artificial intelligence (AI) systems. The theoretical and preliminary exploration of artificial intelligence commenced in the 1930s, but it was not until the renowned Dartmouth Workshop of 1956 that systematic investigation of this field took place (Kline, 2011). Among several contributions, John McCarthy, who was a research fellow at MIT at that time, introduced the phrase "artificial intelligence" as an alternative to "cybernetics." During the initial stages, machine learning (ML) systems were only regarded as a component within a broader artificial intelligence (AI) framework. Since its inception, machine learning has demonstrated a broad range of practical applications that extend beyond the confines originally defined by the AI framework. Currently, the number of autonomous machine learning (ML) systems surpasses the quantity of ML components integrated within artificial intelligence (AI) architectures. The names "AI" and "ML" are frequently used interchangeably, often inappropriately, due to several factors such as their popularity, financial support, or lack of understanding. This practice leads to a state of perplexity among individuals who are not well-versed in these fields. A commonly accepted heuristic is that if a system operates autonomously, it is likely to be classified as having artificial intelligence. If the system engages in classification or prediction through the process of learning, it can be categorised as machine learning. The field of study pertains to the conceptualization and creation of algorithms that possess the ability to acquire knowledge from data in order to generate predictive outcomes. Machine learning models possess the ability to replicate the cognitive process by assimilating knowledge from data and employing it to undertake the processing and analysis of information. The purpose of this technology is to facilitate the automation of cognitive functions. The efficacy of machine learning (ML) is frequently associated with its three primary capabilities: the ability to offer adaptable functional structures capable of capturing nonlinear patterns in data, the capacity to identify pertinent model features without prior specification, and the aptitude to extract information from non-numeric data sources, such as textual data. Nevertheless, a number of recent scholarly investigations, such as the works of Israel *et al.* (2020) and Karolyi and Van Nieuwerburgh (2020), elucidate certain obstacles associated with the application of machine learning (ML) in the realm of finance. The subsequent content presents a concise overview of the aforementioned challenges.

Machine Learning in Finance and Banking

Within the realm of banking, machine learning has the potential to be employed for the purpose of generating useful knowledge by leveraging the vast databases that banks accumulate. Machine learning models have the potential to assist banks in the processing and analysis of many types of data, such as transaction histories, chat logs with bank personnel, and corporate documents. This utilisation of machine learning can enable banks to gain a more comprehensive comprehension of their consumers and internal operations (Shmat, 2022). The topic of finance is commonly perceived as being abundant in relevant data, encompassing various sources such as financial and economic data as well as more contemporary unstructured data like internet news and social media posts. Machine learning in the banking sector enables financial organisations to enhance their fraud detection capabilities, optimise credit underwriting processes, ensure compliance with regulatory requirements, and enhance client interaction. Although the scope of data available for usage in finance is extensive, the time series data commonly employed in this field tends to be somewhat brief when compared to the criteria set by machine learning. A scarcity of time series observations imposes limitations on the size of any model that utilises such data. According to Israel *et al.* (2020), the outcome of this situation is that machine learning systems that require large amounts of data are unable to function at their maximum capacity. In the topic of finance, experimental methods for data generation, commonly employed in other disciplines, are not typically utilised. In the domain of machine learning, specifically in the field of picture recognition, researchers have achieved notable success. One effective approach involves generating a vast dataset of millions of photographs through controlled experiments. These images are then utilised to train the machine learning models. In the field of finance, however, individuals are compelled to patiently await the generation of financial data over a period of time. Machine learning tools play a crucial role in contemporary finance applications. The current forefront of research in finance revolves around three primary issues in machine learning: insufficient data, a low signal-to-noise ratio, and a lack of model interpretability. An increasing body of literature endeavours to identify innovative and imaginative approaches to tackle these challenges (Israel *et al.*, 2020). These advancements have the potential to facilitate a more prominent integration of machine learning in the field of finance in the future.

Benefits of ML

Process Automation in the Field of Corporate Finance

The capacity to optimise and mechanise operational procedures confers many advantages to financial institutions. For instance, enterprises have the capability to employ these technologies in order to streamline mundane activities such as data entry and financial surveillance (Aravind, 2023). This facilitates the concentration of personnel on tasks that necessitate direct human involvement.

The Detection and Prevention of Fraudulent Activities

The increase in the number of transactions, real clients, and integrations will inevitably lead to the emergence of security vulnerabilities. Machine learning techniques seem to be advantageous in instances where banks and other institutions necessitate specialised fraud detection (Aravind, 2023). Banking institutions have the capability to simultaneously monitor a significant number of transactional parameters in real-time for each individual account. The programme does an analysis of historical payment data and evaluates the actions of each cardholder. These models exhibit a high degree of prominence and possess the ability to accurately detect and deter suspicious behaviour. Payoneer, a worldwide financial services provider, offers a global payment system that facilitates online money transactions on a global scale. Based on available data, it is believed that the corporation possesses a client database consisting of millions of entries. Given that the organisation is globally recognised as a registered provider of MasterCard services, the absence of machine-learning applications in the banking sector would result in compromised transaction security.

Portfolio Management

Portfolio management refers to the process of strategically managing a collection of investments, known as a portfolio, in order to achieve specific financial objectives. Portfolio management is an internet-based wealth management solution that leverages statistical analysis and automated algorithms to enhance the performance of clients' assets. Customers provide input regarding their financial objectives, such as the aspiration to accumulate a specific sum of money within a designated timeframe. The robot advisor subsequently allocates existing assets to different investment options and opportunities. The practice of portfolio management entails the establishment and supervision of a carefully chosen array of assets that are in accordance with the investor's enduring financial objectives and capacity for assuming risk. BlackRock Investment Company, a prominent global investment management organisation, provides Aladdin, with an operating system specifically designed and tailored to meet the requirements of investment managers. According to the company's assertions, Aladdin has the capability to leverage machine learning within the realm of financial technology (FinTech). This enables the provision of risk analytics and portfolio management software tools to investment managers in financial institutions. The intended outcome is to facilitate the making of well-informed investment decisions and enhance operational efficiency.

Improving Customer Interactions

One of the most pragmatic uses of machine learning within the realm of banking pertains to client interactions. Finance firms employ machine learning (ML) technologies, such as chatbots, to enhance the client experience by providing immediate assistance and real-time suggestions. Furthermore, insurance companies frequently employ automation techniques to streamline customer acquisition and onboarding procedures, hence enhancing efficiency and convenience.

Customer Engagement

The utilisation of machine learning and AI plays a crucial role in the domain of customer engagement. Internet of Things (IoT) devices produce a substantial amount of data that might be valuable in comprehending client behaviour and preferences. The collected data can then be utilised for the development of tailored marketing campaigns or the enhancement of customer support strategies. Enhancing the total customer experience generally results in increased levels of customer satisfaction and improved customer retention (Zippia, 2023).

Automating Credit Scoring

The process of automating credit scoring involves the utilisation of technological systems and algorithms to assess the creditworthiness of individuals or entities. Machine learning tools have been found to be effective in automating the credit scoring process and enhancing its overall quality. First and foremost, the utilisation of financial assessments reduces the necessity for human labour. Moreover, machine learning algorithms exhibit superiority over classical algorithms by virtue of their capacity to analyse atypical scenarios. This enables the automation of the credit score assignment process for specific circumstances.

Security

The subject of interest pertains to the field of security analysis and portfolio management, specifically focusing on the utilisation of robo-advisors. Robo-advisors represent a prominent illustration of the application of machine learning in the field of finance. The extent of variation in financial services is contingent upon the specific financial institution providing the service. The term "robo-advisor" commonly denotes online platforms that offer investment guidance and assist individuals in establishing and overseeing investment portfolios. The outcome is contingent upon a diverse array of user input preferences. For instance, risk preferences are assessed by gathering data on individuals' decision-making in situations characterised by uncertain conditions.

Prediction of Stock Market Movements

Machine Learning (ML) technology is frequently employed within the finance sector to forecast stock values and exert influence on trading decisions. The operational mechanism involves the utilisation of extensive historical datasets to generate forecasts pertaining to future events. Algorithmic trading is a technique employed in the financial industry to detect patterns and formulate trading strategies with a high degree of precision and efficiency. High-frequency trading (HFT) is employed for the purpose of spotting lucrative trading prospects and promptly executing trades with exceptional velocity.

The Provision of Assistance and Resolution of Inquiries and Concerns from Customers

Effective customer assistance is a crucial component of a thriving financial enterprise. Machine learning in the financial sector facilitates the fulfilment of client requirements through the provision of personalised offers and services. This is achieved by analysing customer behaviour in relation to product utilisation. The primary significance of machine learning in customer retention lies in its ability to enable firms to effectively monitor and predict customer turnover through the analysis of behavioural changes. The cost of acquiring new consumers is significantly higher in comparison to the cost of retaining existing customers. In this particular scenario, machine learning plays a pivotal role in assisting businesses in the identification of consumers who exhibit a propensity to churn, enabling prompt and effective measures to be taken in order to retain them. Machine learning plays a significant role in enhancing client trust and prolonging their engagement, regardless of whether it pertains to individuals who have overlooked a particular service or customers who have encountered unfavourable experiences. Machine learning is an influential instrument that assists financial institutions in enhancing their customer support services. Financial institutions are increasingly adopting machine learning algorithms in order to expedite the customer service process and accurately identify the specific requirements of individual customers. Furthermore, machine learning-powered systems have the ability to acquire knowledge from their past experiences and enhance their performance over time. Additionally, these systems demonstrate the capacity to handle progressively intricate information.

The Prediction of Future Stock Market Performance

The trading sector frequently underestimates predictions regarding stock market volatility, typically regarding them as pseudoscientific. There are individuals who adhere to traditional trading practises and continue to engage in extensive analysis of stock charts utilising Japanese candlestick patterns on a daily basis. Nevertheless, contemporary enterprises possess the ability to formulate approximate conjectures and well-informed projections by leveraging the available knowledge from both the present and the history pertaining to each given stock. Stock technical analysis is a methodology employed to forecast the future price direction of a stock by making an estimated inference based on historical movements and patterns in its stock price. Simultaneously, the predominant approach entails the utilisation of artificial neural networks and algorithms.

Lending Platforms

The utilisation of online lending platforms in conjunction with credit scoring methodologies. Machine learning tools are utilised by the finance industry for the purpose of evaluating loan applications and determining credit scores. Online lending services utilise algorithms to provide real-time data and provide recommendations for loans that are readily available to customers, taking into account their financial history. The application of machine learning in the banking sector has shown considerable potential, with credit scoring emerging as a particularly attractive use case. The assessment examines the customer's ability to make timely payments and their propensity to effectively manage and repay their debts. The global population consists of billions of individuals who do not have access to banking services, commonly referred to as the unbanked population. Additionally, fewer than half of the global population meets the criteria for credit eligibility. Consequently, there exists a significant demand for the development and implementation of credit scoring systems. Machine learning algorithms utilise a diverse range of data points, such as professional background, overall earnings, transactional patterns, and credit records, to make scoring determinations. The mathematical model utilised in this context is founded upon principles derived from accounting and statistical approaches. Consequently, machine learning models have the capability to offer credit score assessments that are more personalised, sensitive, and dependable, thereby expanding credit accessibility to a larger population (Exadel, 2022). In contrast to human scorers, machine learning algorithms possess the ability to assess debtors without being influenced by emotional biases. Moreover, the integration of machine learning in the banking sector enables organisations to mitigate gender, racial, and other forms of conscious or unconscious bias, promoting a more equitable provision of services to a broader range of individuals. The utilisation of machine learning (ML) in credit scoring yields a multitude of advantages, as it enables customers to effortlessly obtain loans through a streamlined digital process, eliminating the need for physical presence or extensive paperwork.

Enhanced Customization / Tailored Promotions

According to Aravind (2023), the utilisation of machine learning techniques can assist banks in discerning trends in customer behaviour, facilitating a more profound comprehension of client preferences and requirements, and facilitating the development of tailored service offerings. The availability of diverse information pertaining to user behaviour enables banks to discern consumers' preferences and their corresponding willingness to pay at any given point in time. For instance, by examining the advertisements that the client has been perusing, it is evident that banks have the capability to provide customised loan options subsequent to a comprehensive assessment of potential hazards and their financial stability. The process of optimising the customer footprint enables banks to identify nuanced patterns in customer behaviour, thereby facilitating the development of personalised experiences for individual clients (Exadel, 2022).

Cost Reduction

The implementation of cost-reduction strategies and risk mitigation measures has resulted in a decrease in operational expenses. By leveraging machine learning and natural language processing (NLP), financial institutions have the capability to automate their back-office activities, enhance the efficiency of document processing workflows, and reduce operational expenses. The application of machine learning techniques in the field of finance has been observed to diminish the requirement for various forms of human labour. The utilisation of automated tools enables the analysis of data and the provision of client assistance (Pletnov, 2023). One example of a neobank is a financial institution that aims to reduce expenses associated with credit history analysis. By utilising a machine learning algorithm, the tool is capable of computing several significant hazards associated with extending loans to certain individuals. This strategy facilitates significant cost savings in relation to routine financial procedures. Moreover, the engagement between individuals yields numerous advantages but is accompanied by a notable drawback. Mistakes continue to be prevalent, and their consequences can be significant in terms of financial or other detrimental impacts. Even seasoned employees are susceptible to making erroneous decisions that can have an impact on the company's responsibility. This is the reason why banks and other financial institutions proactively integrate Machine Learning (ML) and Artificial Intelligence (AI) systems into their operational processes (Exadel, 2022). Robotic

Process Automation (RPA) software is employed to replicate digital operations executed by human operators, thereby mitigating numerous error-prone procedures, such as the inputting of client data derived from forms or contacts. The utilisation of natural language processing and other machine learning technologies, such as robotic process automation bots, enables the effective management of various banking operations.

Algorithmic Trading

Algorithmic trading, often known as automated trading or black-box trading, refers to the use of computer algorithms to execute trades in the financial sector. Machine learning in the field of trading serves as a notable illustration of its successful use within the finance sector (Ariwala, 2023). Algorithmic Trading (AT) has emerged as a dominant force in the global financial markets. Machine learning (ML) systems and models help trading organisations enhance their trading decisions by actively monitoring real-time trade outcomes and news. This allows for the identification of trends that may influence the upward or downward movement of stock values. Machine learning algorithms provide the capability to concurrently analyse numerous data sources, conferring traders with a notable edge over the market average. Algorithmic trading, often known as automated trading or black-box trading, refers to the use of computer algorithms to execute trades in the financial sector. Machine learning in the field of trading serves as a notable illustration of its successful use within the finance sector (Ariwala, 2023). Algorithmic Trading (AT) has emerged as a dominant force in the global financial markets. Machine learning (ML) systems and models help trading organisations enhance their trading decisions by actively monitoring real-time trade outcomes and news. This allows for the identification of trends that may influence the upward or downward movement of stock values. Machine learning algorithms provide the capability to concurrently analyse numerous data sources, conferring traders with a notable edge over the market average.

Settlement and Payments

The integration of machine learning into payment procedures also yields advantages for the payment industry. The utilisation of technology enables payment providers to effectively decrease transaction costs, hence enhancing their ability to attract a larger customer base. One of the benefits of incorporating machine learning into payment systems is the ability to enhance payment routing by considering factors such as pricing, functionality, performance, and other relevant variables (Pletnov, 2023). Through the utilisation of diverse data sources, machine learning systems possess the capability to effectively distribute traffic to the most optimal amalgamation of factors. This functionality enables financial institutions to provide optimal outcomes to merchants in accordance with their individual goals. In the contemporary landscape, a plethora of machine learning applications tailored for the financial sector have emerged, offering firms a valuable means to address prevalent challenges and yield substantial benefits (Exadel, 2022). The utilisation of machine learning in payment processing enables payment providers to discern whether a transaction should proceed or be initially directed to a two-step verification page.

Financial Monitoring

The practice of financial monitoring refers to the systematic and ongoing observation and analysis of financial activities inside an organisation or individual's financial system. Machine learning algorithms have the potential to greatly boost network security. Data scientists consistently engage in the development of training systems aimed at detecting indicators, such as money laundering techniques, with the objective of mitigating such activities through the implementation of financial monitoring measures. There is a strong likelihood that machine learning technologies will play a pivotal role in driving the development of highly sophisticated cybersecurity networks in the future.

Process Automation

Process automation refers to the use of technology and software to streamline and automate repetitive tasks and processes inside an organisation. Machine Learning-driven solutions enable financial institutions to fully substitute manual labour by automating repetitive processes through intelligent process automation, hence enhancing corporate productivity. Process automation in finance using machine learning encompasses many techniques such as chatbots, paperwork automation, and employee training gamification. According to Ariwala (2023), the utilisation of this technology allows finance organisations to enhance their customer experience, minimise expenses, and expand the scope of their services. Moreover, the utilisation of Machine Learning technology enables seamless access to data, proficient interpretation of behaviours, and accurate identification and tracking of trends. This technology has the potential to be effectively applied to customer support systems, enabling them to emulate human-like interactions and effectively address a wide range of individual consumer inquiries.

Secure Transactions

Machine Learning algorithms demonstrate a high level of proficiency in identifying instances of transactional fraud through the analysis of vast quantities of data points, which often elude human detection. Moreover, machine learning (ML) also has the capability to decrease the occurrence of erroneous rejections and enhance the accuracy of instantaneous approvals (Ariwala, 2023). Typically, these models are constructed based on the clientele's online behaviour and transactional records. In addition to its high accuracy in detecting fraudulent behaviour, machine learning (ML)-powered technology possesses the capability to promptly identify suspicious account activity and proactively prevent fraud in real-time, as opposed to retroactively discovering such incidents after the occurrence of the crime. Credit card fraud prevention is widely recognised as one of the most successful applications of machine learning. Banks typically possess monitoring systems that have been trained using historical payment data (Ariwala, 2023). The processes of algorithm training, validation, and backtesting rely on extensive datasets of credit card transaction information. Machine learning algorithms that utilise artificial intelligence have the capability to accurately classify occurrences as either fraudulent or non-fraudulent, enabling the timely prevention of fraudulent transactions.

Risk Management

Risk management is a systematic and structured approach to identifying, assessing, and mitigating any risks that may impact an organization's objectives. By employing machine learning methodologies, banks and financial institutions have the ability to effectively mitigate risk levels through the comprehensive analysis of extensive datasets. In contrast to conventional approaches that typically focus on fundamental factors like credit scores, Machine Learning (ML) has the capacity to analyse substantial quantities of personal data in order to mitigate risk (Ariwala, 2023). Machine learning technology offers a range of valuable insights that can be utilised by banking and financial services organisations to inform their decision-making processes. One illustrative instance entails the utilisation of machine learning algorithms to access diverse data sources in order to evaluate loan applicants and award corresponding risk scores. Machine learning algorithms have the potential to accurately forecast customers who are at a higher likelihood of defaulting on their loans. This valuable insight can assist organisations in reevaluating and modifying loan terms for individual customers.

Financial Advisory

According to Ariwala (2023), there exist a range of budget management applications that utilise machine learning technology. These applications have the capability to provide consumers with the advantage of receiving highly specialised and targeted financial advice and guidance. Machine Learning techniques enable users to monitor their daily expenditures through mobile applications while also facilitating data analysis to discern spending patterns and discover potential areas for cost reduction. Another noteworthy trend that is quickly gaining prominence in this particular context is the utilisation of Robo-advisors. Operating in a manner similar to traditional financial consultants, these entities especially focus on catering to investors who have little financial resources, including individuals and small to medium-sized firms, who are seeking to effectively manage their finances. ML-based robo-advisors possess the capability to employ conventional data processing approaches in order to generate financial portfolios and solutions encompassing trading, investments, retirement plans, and other related aspects for their clientele.

Customer Data Management

Customer data management refers to the process of organising, storing, and maintaining customer information in a systematic and efficient manner. It involves the collection, analysis, and utilisation of data. The efficient administration of data is of paramount importance in the banking and financial sectors, as it is considered the most critical resource for these institutions (Ariwala, 2023). This underscores the significance of effective data management in driving the growth and achievement of corporate objectives. The extensive quantity and varied structure of financial data, ranging from mobile communications and social media activity to transactional details and market data, provide a significant obstacle for financial experts to manually analyse and interpret. The incorporation of machine learning methodologies for the purpose of handling substantial quantities of data has the potential to yield improvements in operational effectiveness, as well as the ability to derive meaningful insights from the data. Artificial Intelligence (AI) and Machine Learning (ML) technologies, including data analytics, data mining, and Natural Language Processing (NLP), facilitate the extraction of useful insights from data, hence enhancing corporate profitability (Ariwala, 2023). A compelling illustration of this phenomenon may be observed in the utilisation of machine learning algorithms for the purpose of analysing the impact of market changes and specific financial trends based on client financial data.

Decision-Making

The process of decision-making is a cognitive process that involves selecting a course of action. Machine Learning algorithms have the potential to be employed by banking and financial institutions for the analysis of both structured and unstructured data (Ariwala, 2023). For instance, the analysis of customer requests, interactions on social media platforms, and internal corporate processes enables the identification of patterns that can be both beneficial and possibly risky. This analysis aids in the evaluation of risks and facilitates customers in making accurate and informed decisions. According to Aravind (2023), the utilisation of Machine Learning (ML) offers banks the opportunity to leverage their ability to efficiently and accurately analyse vast quantities of data. This capability enables banks to make critical choices more often and with reduced levels of risk.

Enhancing Customer Service Levels

According to Ariwala (2023), clients can utilise an intelligent chatbot to obtain comprehensive assistance in various areas, such as determining their monthly expenses, assessing their eligibility for loans, identifying suitable insurance plans within their financial means, and accessing more relevant information. Moreover, there are various machine learning-based applications that, when integrated with a payment system, have the capability to analyse accounts and enable clients to effectively accumulate and increase their financial resources. According to Ariwala (2023), advanced machine learning algorithms can be employed to examine user behaviour and generate tailored offers. For instance, a potential investor seeking to allocate funds towards a financial strategy may derive advantages from a customised investment proposal following the machine learning algorithm's evaluation of their current financial circumstances.

Customer Retention Program

The implementation of a customer retention programme is a strategic initiative aimed at enhancing customer loyalty and reducing customer churn. Credit card firms have the capability to employ Machine Learning (ML) technology in order to forecast clients who are at a higher risk of attrition, and afterwards implement targeted strategies to retain these individuals. According to Ariwala (2023), by analysing user personal data and transactional activity, it becomes feasible to make accurate predictions about user behaviour and tailor offers, particularly for these clients. The proposed methodology involves the implementation of a predictive model for binary classification in order to identify consumers who are at risk. Subsequently, a recommender model is employed to select the most suitable card offers that can be utilised to retain these customers.

Marketing

The field of marketing encompasses various strategies and techniques employed by organisations to promote their products or services. The capacity of AI and ML models to generate precise forecasts by leveraging historical patterns renders them highly effective as marketing instruments. According to Ariwala (2023), the utilisation of machine learning algorithms can contribute to the development of a comprehensive marketing plan for financial institutions by examining mobile app usage, web activity, and prior ad campaign outcomes.

The Identification and Classification of Anomalies within a Given Dataset

Anomaly detection poses significant challenges within the asset-serving segment of financial organisations. Anomalies may arise as a consequence of accidents, instances of ineptitude, or system mistakes within routine operational procedures. In the fintech sector, the identification of anomalies is of utmost importance due to their potential association with illicit practices such as account hijacking, fraudulent activities, network breaches, or money laundering. These actions might lead to unforeseen consequences and must be promptly detected. There are various approaches to tackling the issue of anomaly detection, with machine learning being one of the most viable methods. According to Exadel (2022), machine learning-based anti-fraud solutions in the field of banking possess the capability to detect nuanced occurrences and associations within user behaviour. The system conducts real-time comparisons of several factors and possesses the capability to analyse extensive datasets in order to determine the probability of fraudulent transactions.

Risk Management and Prevention

Machine Learning (ML) technology is frequently employed within the banking industry to facilitate investment decision-making processes through the identification of hazards using historical data and probability statistics. By employing machine learning methodologies, banks and financial institutions have the ability to effectively mitigate risk levels through the comprehensive analysis of extensive data sources. In contrast to conventional approaches that typically focus on fundamental factors like credit scores, Machine Learning (ML) has the capacity to analyse substantial quantities of personal data in order to mitigate risk (Ariwala, 2023). Additionally, it can be utilised to assess potential consequences and formulate methods for mitigating risks. The utilisation of machine learning enables decision-makers to develop more informed strategies by effectively modelling the response of a bank to certain economic conditions. Machine learning technology has been found to offer valuable insights to banking and financial services organisations, enabling them to make informed decisions (Ariwala, 2023). One illustrative instance entails the utilisation of machine learning algorithms to access diverse data sources in order to evaluate loan applicants and award corresponding risk scores. Machine learning algorithms have the potential to accurately forecast clients who are at a higher likelihood of defaulting on their loans, enabling corporations to reconsider and modify loan terms for individual customers.

Enhanced Assessment of Investments

The investment valuation procedure encompasses a series of intricate computations. The approach entails fostering collaboration among diverse teams accountable for distinct facets of investment asset management, product expertise, and portfolio oversight. Exadel (2022) suggests that it might be prudent for these teams to contemplate alternative strategies for investment. The Machine Learning (ML) approach proposed involves the development of an application capable of efficiently handling substantial volumes of data from diverse sources in real time. This application would simultaneously acquire knowledge about biases and preferences related to risk tolerance, investments, and time horizons.

Improved Efficiency in Operations

The act of allocating resources, such as money or time, with the expectation of generating more money and output. Machine learning technology has the potential to enhance the operational efficiency of investment organisations. Trading organisations utilise machine learning algorithms to concurrently monitor trade outcomes, financial news, prices, and various data resources in order to identify trends that influence the fluctuations in the values of financial documents (Exadel, 2022). Algorithms have the capability to execute deals at prices that are deemed reasonable, thereby mitigating the occurrence of human errors that might potentially lead to substantial financial losses amounting to millions of dollars. Machine learning has the additional benefit of enhancing accessibility to financial markets through the utilisation of automated robo-advisors. These robo-advisors are capable of generating investment proposals automatically, taking into account the specific preferences of individual customers. These advisors possess the ability to construct customised investment portfolios tailored to individual customers' needs, facilitating the achievement of various financial objectives such as retirement planning, savings accumulation, and safeguarding against the erosive effects of inflation.

Enhanced Loan and Credit Decision-Making

One further advantage of using machine learning and artificial intelligence services in the banking sector is the enhancement of loan and credit decision-making processes, leading to increased safety and informed judgements by financial institutions. Numerous financial institutions presently exhibit proficiency in leveraging credit history, banking transactions, and client references as means of assessing the creditworthiness of both corporate entities and individuals (Exadel, 2022). Moreover, machine learning-based systems have the capability to analyse patterns and behaviours in order to assess the creditworthiness of customers with minimal credit histories. One potential concern associated with Machine Learning (ML)-powered systems pertains to the presence of bias-related concerns, which can be attributed to the training process of ML models. Nevertheless, numerous institutions exhibit a strong inclination towards the use of machine learning systems within the banking sector, with the primary objective of mitigating prejudice and incorporating ethical considerations into their machine learning training methodologies.

Unstructured and Large Data

The application of machine learning in the field of finance has facilitated the process of extracting and analysing unstructured data from various sources, such as contracts or financial reports. The utilisation of big data analysis has become vital in comprehending client behaviour and trends. Machine learning and Artificial Intelligence (AI) have the potential to facilitate the comprehension of extensive datasets, discern patterns within them, and generate predictive insights. This strategy can provide a competitive advantage by enabling individuals or organisations to make more efficient and effective decisions compared to their competition.

The Detection of Fraudulent Activities and Adherence to Regulatory Requirements

Machine learning enables financial institutions to actively monitor consumer behaviour, detect anomalies in real time, minimise the occurrence of false positives, and mitigate instances of fraudulent activity. The central concept revolves around the utilisation of machine learning systems to effectively analyse vast volumes of data through the application of diverse algorithms, hence enabling the identification of fraudulent activities. In the context of regulatory compliance, machine learning virtual assistants are employed by banks to oversee transactions, observe consumer behaviour, and record data in supplementary compliance and regulatory systems, hence reducing overall risk (Exadel, 2022). Financial systems are frequently utilised by individuals to engage in money laundering or perpetrate acts of deception against others. These activities typically exhibit distinct indicators. The application of machine learning in the field of finance enhances the likelihood of early detection of the aforementioned difficulties. In a matter of minutes, these systems possess the capacity to process a volume of data that would challenge human cognitive capacities for an extended period of several days (Pletnov, 2023). This technique facilitates the mitigation of adverse inclinations pertaining to the financial industry. The extensive array of benefits associated with Machine Learning (ML) in the banking sector is seemingly boundless. Presented below are merely a handful of the most prevalent rationales for banks to implement ML methodologies within their operational processes. Machine-learning models acquire knowledge by discerning and recognising patterns. These patterns facilitate comprehension of typical behaviour and enhance the identification of potentially illicit behaviours, such as money laundering or insider trading.

The Automation of the Trade Settlement Procedure

The process of trade settlement has the potential to consume a significant amount of time and is susceptible to errors. Occasionally, trading transactions may experience failure. According to Ariwala (2023), the implementation of Machine Learning technology in finance organisations enables the automation of repetitive operations, leading to increased corporate efficiency through intelligent process automation. Process automation in the field of finance utilising machine learning encompasses several applications such as chatbots, paperwork automation, and employee training gamification. This facilitates finance organisations in enhancing their customer experience, minimising expenses, and expanding their service capabilities. In the pre-machine learning era of finance, personnel within financial institutions were responsible for manually handling trade failures, which involved the tasks of processing, identifying the underlying causes, and subsequently resolving the encountered issues. The utilisation of machine learning technologies has streamlined this labor-intensive procedure by automatically identifying and highlighting problems, as well as providing suggestions for their solutions. Moreover, the utilisation of Machine Learning technology enables seamless data accessibility, efficient interpretation of behaviours, and accurate identification and tracking of trends (Ariwala, 2023). This technology has the potential to be effectively employed in customer support systems, functioning in a manner akin to human agents, thereby addressing and resolving a wide range of individual consumer inquiries.

The Appraisal and Management of Assets

Asset managers utilise machine learning (ML) and artificial intelligence (AI) techniques to assess and oversee various types of assets, such as stocks and bonds. The utilisation of data-driven decision-making processes aids in mitigating the potential for human error resulting from confirmation bias or loss aversion.

Financial Monitoring

The practice of financial monitoring involves the systematic observation and analysis of financial activities and transactions inside an organisation or individual's financial system. The utilisation of machine learning algorithms has the potential to greatly augment network security. Data scientists are consistently engaged in the development and refinement of training systems aimed at identifying indicators, such as money laundering tactics, that can be effectively mitigated through the use of financial monitoring measures (Ariwala, 2023). There is a strong likelihood that machine learning technologies will play a significant role in driving the development of highly advanced cybersecurity networks in the future.

Enhancing Time Efficiency

Certain conventional banking practices exhibit a lack of expediency. For instance, the act of obtaining a loan entails a protracted procedure that necessitates the evaluation of one's credit history and the completion of substantial documentation. According to Pletnov (2023), the utilisation of machine learning techniques facilitates the automation of the aforementioned operations. These frameworks enable contemporary neobanks to efficiently and expeditiously disburse loans, bypassing the need for protracted verification processes. The utilisation of machine learning facilitates a more expedited analysis of financial data. With the use of contemporary high-speed processors, it is possible to expedite the analysis of vast amounts of information that would otherwise take people thousands of years to process, completing the task within a matter of hours.

Challenges of ML in Banking and Finance

While machine learning offers various advantages in the banking industry, it also presents a range of obstacles. One of the foremost obstacles lies in the integrity of the data. According to Ng and Shah (2020), in order to achieve accurate outcomes, techniques for machine learning necessitate the use of high-quality data. The interpretability and comprehensibility of machine learning models provide a significant obstacle for financial institutions in elucidating their decision-making procedures to regulatory bodies or clients. The establishment of openness and accessibility in machine learning algorithms is of utmost importance in fostering confidence and upholding accountability. This post presents a comprehensive examination of interpretable machine learning and the strategies employed to establish trust in machine learning models. Within the domain of banking, it is not uncommon for data to exhibit characteristics like disorderliness, incompleteness, or inconsistency, all of which have the potential to undermine the precision of algorithmic outputs. Hence, the process of data cleansing and preparation holds significant importance when incorporating machine learning techniques within the banking sector (Konczyk, 2019). One further obstacle that arises is the absence of transparency inside machine learning algorithms. It is imperative for financial institutions to provide a comprehensive account of the decision-making process employed by their algorithms, particularly in instances where such judgments have a direct impact on their clientele. The efficacy of machine learning algorithms is intrinsically linked to the quality of the data employed for their training. The field of quantitative finance places great importance on the quality of data, as even minor flaws or biases within the data can yield substantial ramifications.

The introduction of artificial intelligence and machine learning technologies expands the potential for cyber threats and introduces novel and distinctive cyber dangers. In addition to conventional cyber dangers arising from human or software faults, artificial intelligence and machine learning systems are susceptible to emerging and innovative threats. The aforementioned concerns mostly revolve around the manipulation of data at various stages within the lifecycle of artificial intelligence and machine learning, with the intention of exploiting the inherent limitations present in AI and ML algorithms (Comiter, 2019). This sort of manipulation enables malicious actors to circumvent detection mechanisms, leading to erroneous decision-making by AI and ML systems and the extraction of sensitive information. ML models necessitate ongoing supervision to ensure the consistent detection and quick management of assaults, given their intricate nature and potential ramifications for financial sector institutions (Ng & Shah, 2020). Machine learning models possess a black-box characteristic because of their intricate computations, which are challenging to comprehend. Hence, there is a restricted comprehension of the output. One notable deficiency for financial institutions is the lack of suitable training among data scientists and machine learning modellers. This deficiency can lead to the absence of model explainability, which in turn can result in customer attrition. Overfitting is a prevalent concern in the field of machine learning, wherein models exhibit excessive complexity and are excessively tailored to the training data. Consequently, this phenomenon gives rise to limited capacity for extrapolation to novel datasets and may engender imprecise prognostications. In order to mitigate the issue of overfitting, it is imperative for financial institutions to guarantee that their machine-learning models undergo proper training and testing procedures. The user's text could be rewritten to be more academic as follows: "The user's text In order to tackle these concerns, it is customary to utilise suitable data pretreatment methodologies, including data normalisation and feature selection, while also giving due consideration to the model's complexity and regularisation procedures (Ng & Shah, 2020). In addition, conducting thorough testing and validation of the model's output is advantageous in order to ascertain its ability to effectively generalise to novel and unfamiliar data. The ML workflow encompasses a diverse range of procedures, such as data analysis, data manipulation, model training, validation, testing, and monitoring, among others. As the volume of data increases and processing capabilities expand, it becomes imperative to restructure machine learning algorithms. Consequently, continuous monitoring and maintenance have a critical role in this context. Consequently, this may be a daunting challenge.

Future of Machine Learning in Finance and Banking

First and foremost, it provides significant prospects for customization. Through the examination of individual data, it is possible to generate distinct offers tailored specifically for bank customers. This approach presents an optimal method for enhancing customer loyalty. Additionally, machine learning enhances the efficacy of anti-fraud measures. Artificial Intelligence (AI) systems possess the capability to acquire the ability to identify diverse forms of fraudulent activities, and in certain instances, they can even uncover novel fraudulent schemes. The aforementioned factor plays a key role in enhancing customer security. Finally, it is our belief that machine learning presents a chance to develop computerised assistance systems. Applications that utilise models like ChatGPT have the potential to reduce the need for human labour in the field of customer assistance. The utilisation of advanced machines capable of effectively responding to intricate cues holds the potential to effectively address a wide range of challenging scenarios pertaining to banking services.

Implications

The purpose of this section is to provide recommendations and discuss the managerial consequences of implementing machine learning in the financial and banking management approach based on the identified themes. In conclusion, the provided data suggests that the implementation of machine learning in the banking sector is a prudent and valuable investment. This presents a potential avenue for the introduction of novel services to clients while concurrently mitigating various risks. For individuals seeking to engage in investment activities within this domain, it is advisable to seek out reputable firms that have a track record of expertise in the financial sector. The utilisation of machine learning in the financial sector by managers yields both advantageous and disadvantageous effects on leverage, liquidity, and maturity transformation. On the one hand, it has the potential to improve liquidity and risk management, fostering a more diverse risk-sharing framework within the financial system. Moreover, it has the potential to decrease dependence on financial borrowing from banks. Conversely, the utilisation of machine learning has the ability to heighten risks by enabling more stringent liquidity buffers, increased leverage, and accelerated maturity transformation. Consequently, this may have a potentially adverse effect on capital or margins. To effectively anticipate the emergence of novel threats, it is imperative to enhance the organization's knowledge of the security implications of Artificial Intelligence (AI). Facilitate collaboration with diverse stakeholders to effectively address and mitigate cyber threats. The establishment of strong governance frameworks and accountability systems is of utmost importance when implementing machine learning models in decision-making contexts that carry significant consequences, such as credit access assessment or investment portfolio allocation. Financial market participants who employ machine learning techniques now depend on the existing governance and oversight structures in place to regulate the utilisation of this technology. According to the International Organisation of Securities Commissions, AI-based algorithms are not regarded as fundamentally distinct from conventional algorithms. The current governance frameworks that pertain to models can serve as a foundation for the creation or modification of Machine Learning (ML) endeavours, as numerous issues and hazards linked to Artificial Intelligence (AI) are also relevant to other model categories. The expansion of the scope will also result in modifications to the risk classification procedures employed by actors. The findings indicate that discussion forums provide organisations with a valuable means to choose the most effective approach for classifying risks, as there are multiple methods to do this task. In order to comprehensively handle various risks, it is imperative to incorporate all pertinent parties in these deliberations. Finally, the dynamic and ever-changing characteristics of Machine Learning (ML) products will necessitate modifications in the evaluation process of the system. Given the dynamic nature of AI-ML products, it becomes imperative to incorporate a periodic evaluation of the impact of their output into the risk management process. Therefore, it is imperative for managers to create appropriate procedures to monitor the progression of products.

CONCLUSION

The integration of Artificial Intelligence (AI) and Machine Learning (ML) in the banking sector represents a significant paradigm shift, promising enhanced safety, innovation, and efficiency within bank services. The presence of a substantial volume of data is a critical component in the field of finance. The users engage in a significant number of transactions on a daily basis, thereby offering valuable insights into their behavioural patterns. Historically, banks and financial institutions possessed limited capacity to analyse such information. General trends in the data can be identified, whereas the more intricate aspects necessitate substantial computational resources. Machine learning in the field of finance effectively addresses the aforementioned issue. Machines possess a greater degree of freedom in conducting data analysis compared to humans. These individuals possess the ability to efficiently and rapidly assess huge quantities of information without experiencing fatigue. Through the examination of transaction data, machine learning algorithms are capable of generating accurate and reliable statistical insights, encompassing even the most intricate events. It is possible to acquire insights into both the general purchasing preferences of a community and individual customer profiles, enabling the identification of optimal selling periods for specific products. In summary, machine learning facilitates the optimisation of financial data analysis by enhancing its precision and focus. The utilisation of machine learning technologies in the banking sector has the potential to enhance sales by fostering meaningful engagement. This can be achieved by initially focusing on high-value instances and subsequently expanding the implementation across other organisations. The integration of AI solutions has emerged as a fundamental element of novel enterprise value propositions, transcending its role as a mere supplement to existing processes. It has now evolved into a pivotal strategic imperative for achieving success within the global banking industry.

FUTURE RESEARCH DIRECTION

Although there has been considerable study conducted on the utilisation of machine learning in the field of record management, its implementation remains inadequate and inconsistent across different domains of risk management and risk approaches. There are other areas within bank risk management, as previously said, that might greatly benefit from more investigation into the application of machine learning techniques to effectively solve specific challenges.

REFERENCES

Aravind, R. (2023). Benefits of Machine Learning in the Banking Industry. Available from: https://www.linkedin.com/pulse/benefits-machine-learning-banking-industry-aravind-raghunathan#:~:text=With%20machine%20learning%20in%20banking,compliance%2C%20and%20strengthen%20customer%20engagement.

Ariwala, P. (2023). 12 Ways AI and Machine Learning are Transforming Finance. Available from: https://marutitech.com/ai-and-ml-in-finance/.

Deloitte University Press. (2017). Global Risk Management Survey, 10th ed. Deloitte University Press: Available from: https://www2.deloitte.com/tr/en/pages/risk/articles/global-risk-management-survey-10th-ed.html.

Exadel, (2022). How Machine Learning is Used in Finance and Banking. Available from: https://exadel.com/news/how-machine-learning-is-used-in-finance-and-banking/.

Israel, R., Kelly, B.T., Moskowitz, T.J. (2020). Can machines 'learn' finance? *Social Science Research Network.*
[http://dx.doi.org/10.2139/ssrn.3624052]

Karolyi, G.A., Van Nieuwerburgh, S. (2020). New methods for the cross-section of returns. *Rev. Financ. Stud., 33*(5), 1879-1890.
[http://dx.doi.org/10.1093/rfs/hhaa019]

Kline, R.R. (2011). Cybernetics, automata studies and the dartmouth conference on artifcial intelligence. *IEEE Annals of the History of Computing, October–December.*. IEEE Computer Society.

Konczyk, J. (2019). *AI for Finance.*. Packt Publishing.

Leo, M., Sharma, S., Maddulety, K. (2019). Machine Learning in Banking Risk Management: A Literature Review. *Risks, 7*(1), 29.

[http://dx.doi.org/10.3390/risks7010029]

Metric Stream. (2018). The Chief Risk Officer's Role in 2018 and Beyond Managing the Challenges and Opportunities of a Digital Era New Roles of the CRO. Available from: https://www.metricstream.com/insights/chiefrisk-officer-role-2018.htm.

Ng, J., Shah, S. (2020). Hands-On Artificial Intelligence for Banking. *Packt Publishing,* 240.

Oliver Wyman. (2017). Next Generation Risk Management. Available from: https://www.oliverwyman.com/content/dam/oliver-wyman/v2/publications/2017/aug/Next_Generation_Risk_Management_Targeting_A-Technology_Dividend.pdf.

Pletnov, A. (2023). Machine Learning in Finance: Benefits and Use Cases. Available from: https://keenethics.com/blog/machine-learning-in-finance.

Shmat, D. (2022). Machine learning in banking: 8 use cases and implementation guidelines. Available from: https://www.itransition.com/machine-learning/banking.

Van Liebergen, B. (2017). Machine Learning: A Revolution in Risk Management and Compliance? *J. Financ. Transform., 45*, 60-67.

Zippia. (2023). Data Scientist Education Requirements, Available from: https://www.zippia.com/data-scientist-jobs/education/.

CHAPTER 8

Banking on IoT in Transforming Financial Services for the Digital Age

Victoria Manu[1,*]

[1] *Accountancy Department, Valley View University, Oyibi-Ghana*

Abstract: Financial and banking services sector plays a crucial role in the economic development of many nations, serving as a foundation for growth. Information Technology (IT) plays a vital role in facilitating the management of these services and streamlining operations for banking institutions, enabling them to expand their reach and efficiency. The Internet of Things (IoT) is a component of intelligent infrastructure, and the banking sector is among the possible domains that can benefit significantly from the use of IoT technologies. Therefore, this chapter examines the use of the Internet of Things (IoTs) within the finance and banking industries. This study examines the advantages and obstacles associated with the implementation of Internet of Things (IoT) technology in the banking industry. The banking business is experiencing a notable shift towards digitalization, hence enhancing convenience for users. The Internet of Things (IoT) is a significant component of the ongoing rapid transformation towards the future of banking. It is crucial for both consumers and financial institutions to adjust and align themselves with the emerging trends in retail and mobile banking.

Keywords: Banking, Finance, Fintech, Internet of things, Technology.

INTRODUCTION

The field of financial technology (Fintech) has experienced significant growth since 2018, as evidenced by the substantial increase in international investments, which have reached a staggering amount of approximately 60 billion USD (Arslanian and Fischer, 2019). It is projected that the monetary transactions facilitated by smart wearable devices alone will reach a total of 75 billion USD by the year 2025. Fintech encompasses a range of novel approaches to financial exchanges and banking services that are facilitated by the integration of advanced

* **Corresponding author Victoria Manu:** Accountancy Department, Valley View University, Oyibi-Ghana;
E-mail: victoria.manu@stu.edu.gh

Abdul-Razak Abubakari, Mohammed Majeed, Nurideen Alhassan and Jonas Yomboi (Eds.)

computer interaction, data science, social networking, and Artificially Intelligent (AI) technologies. Fintech predominantly depends on several technological advancements such as the Internet of Things (IoT), blockchain, Artificial Intelligence (AI), data analytics, and 5G and Beyond (B5G) to enhance the customer experience, ensure security, and improve efficiency in the provision of financial services. The authors, Olsen and Tomlin (2020), provide a comprehensive analysis of the technological aspects associated with Industry 4.0 as well as an examination of the potential research prospects and obstacles within this domain. The technologies that were specifically discussed encompass additive manufacturing, the Internet of Things, blockchain, sophisticated robotics, and artificial intelligence. The term "Internet of Things" (IoT) denotes the convergence of physical devices that are interconnected *via* the Internet, despite their inherent lack of physical connectivity. It is important to acknowledge that the growth of the Internet of Things (IoT) is considered a significant scientific and technological trend within the context of Industry 4.0 (Baranovskyi, 2020). The emergence of the Internet of Things (IoT) is often regarded as a significant technological revolution with far-reaching implications across several domains of human existence. This technology enables the expansion of chances for the collection, processing, and distribution of data, which can then be transformed into information or knowledge. Hence, the development of the Internet of Things (IoT) is substantiated at the organisational level, as indicated by a single entity. It is evident that the governments of highly developed nations are actively engaged in investing in research and development within the Internet of Things (IoT) domain. According to Miskiewicz (2020), the categorization of literary sources reveals variations in the extent of Internet of Things (IoT) advancement across different regions globally. The primary components of this system consist primarily of adaptable equipment capable of perceiving and acquiring data in various contexts, irrespective of the presence of human beings. The relevance of the Internet of Things (IoT) in the domains of finance and business stems from the proliferation of smart devices and easily accessible connectivity. This technological landscape enables businesses to engage in data-driven analytics and make well-informed decisions, a capability that was previously unprecedented (Avasalcai, Tsigkanos, & Dustdar, 2019; Mick, Tourani, & Misra, 2018; Yomboi *et al.* , 2021). This encompasses a wide range of gadgets, such as smartphones, refrigerators, washing machines, lighting, video sensors, cameras, wearable devices, and other machine components, such as the jet engine of an aeroplane or the drill of an oil rig. According to Atzori, Iera, and Morabito (2010), the concept under consideration exhibits a broad range of associations within the context of human society.

Emerging technologies, such as the Internet of Things (IoT) and blockchain, have the potential to optimise the transmission of information within the supply chain.

These technologies can mitigate risks associated with supply chain finance (SCF) and provide support to conventional banking institutions (Wamba and Queiroz, 2020). The utilisation of the Internet of Things (IoT) has become a prominent aspect of consumer product innovation. There is ongoing discourse around wearable electronics, smart cities, and other related topics within the realm of the Internet of Things (IoT). However, it remains uncertain if the prevailing enthusiasm for IoT mostly stems from exaggerated claims or genuine interest in the underlying banking and financial frameworks. Therefore, this chapter examines the use of the Internet of Things (IoTs) within the finance and banking industries. This study examines the advantages and obstacles associated with the implementation of Internet of Things (IoT) technology in the banking industry.

Contribution

This chapter makes a valuable contribution to the existing literature by providing empirical evidence that supports the significance of new technologies, specifically the Internet of Things (IoTs), in the domain of banking and finance. Additionally, the evaluation offers significant insights for practitioners seeking to enhance the effectiveness of practices and approaches in the realm of fintech concerns within the banking and financial sectors.

LITERATURE

Internet of Things

The concept of the Internet of Things (IoT) refers to a collection of diverse interconnected devices that are linked by various communication interfaces and sensors. This connectivity allows for the identification, location, and manipulation of these objects. In the era of digitalization, a predominant emphasis among organisations lies in the provision of customised and individualised advice and services to their clientele *via* applications or online platforms. In order to enhance customer service, numerous financial institutions, such as banks, investment advisers, and insurance firms, have undertaken process redesign initiatives incorporating machine learning and other AI technologies (Kumari *et al.* , 2020). These technological advancements facilitate the provision of uninterrupted services, such as electronic commerce, electronic health, electronic banking, and so on, to the final consumers. The Internet of Things (IoT) is expected to have a significant impact on various industries, including banking, financial planning, insurance, autos, and healthcare. Its integration into these sectors has the potential to enhance the delivery of services and improve overall performance. Various examples of data collection and connectivity in different industries may be observed. For instance, the insurance business utilises smart sensors, while shopping terminals employ RFID technology. Additionally, mobile banking services, industrial sensors, and healthcare wearable devices are also notable examples. These technologies facilitate the collection and transmission of data to the Internet, where it can be stored, processed, and analysed (Marafie *et al.*, 2018). The Internet of Things (IoT) devices will gather diverse sets of data from users, encompassing information such as geographical position, credit card usage patterns, health-related data, and driving behaviours. These data have significant value for organisations seeking to enhance their business operations and promotional strategies. Insurance, banking, and financial institutions are encouraged to engage with the Internet of Things (IoT) in order to foster the development of novel financial products.

Internet of Things in Finance and Banking

The concept of IoT in the banking sector refers to the interrelated systems of IoT devices that gather, transmit, and facilitate the analysis of data in either a cloud or on-premise server, with the aim of enhancing the banking experience for both customers and financial professionals (Pandey, 2023). The utilisation of Internet of Things (IoT) technology and its associated devices has the potential to significantly alter customers' experiences inside the banking environment. Moreover, the Internet has undergone significant evolution throughout the past few decades, transitioning from a mere assemblage of interconnected gadgets. The Internet of Things (IoT) holds considerable importance within the financial industry, exhibiting the capacity to revolutionise the realms of finance and banking. The implementation of the Internet of Things (IoT) in the banking sector has proven to be advantageous in terms of time efficiency due to its ability to streamline data gathering and facilitate the transmission of large volumes of data (Grivas, Schürch, & Giovanoli, 2016). The Internet of Things (IoT) also facilitates the enhancement of customer experience and the fortification of the overall security system within financial institutions. Customers have the ability to engage in a wide range of transactions without the need to physically visit banking institutions. Additionally, they can utilise self-assisted customer care services, which employ virtual assistants to address and handle any issues that may arise.

When confronted with a novel concept or object, it is imperative to identify and comprehend the persuasive justifications for its necessity. Prior to embarking on the development of an IoT solution for the banking sector or any other Fintech enterprise, it is important to acquire a comprehensive comprehension of the significance of IoT within the banking industry (Miskiewicz, 2020). The proliferation of Internet of Things (IoT) devices has experienced a significant expansion, with the number of such gadgets increasing from millions to billions. Additionally, there has been a notable increase in the duration of time that users dedicate to using these devices. The Internet of Things (IoT) refers to a network of networked devices that have the capability to gather and transmit data wirelessly, hence facilitating the convergence of virtual realms. The integration of remote and digital-based Internet of Things (IoT) devices has led to the regular occurrence of data transfers in many contexts (Pandey, 2023). In order to acquire a substantial volume of data, these devices have the capability to transmit signals to both the server and other devices. The advantages of implementing Internet of Things (IoT) technology in the banking sector have garnered significant interest from organisations globally (Miskiewicz, 2020). Numerous sectors, including healthcare, retail, and financial services, are currently exploring strategies to leverage the potential of the Internet of Things (IoT) in order to achieve remarkable financial gains through commercial endeavours.

The notion of the "Internet of Things" (IoT) involves the interconnection of all entities within the global domain to the Internet. This suggests the expansion of the Internet's functionalities beyond traditional devices such as smartphones and computers, encompassing a diverse array of objects, processes, and settings. The implementation of Internet of Things (IoT) technology allows enterprises to enhance their comprehension of operational processes and exert authority over their surrounding environment (Miskiewicz, 2020).

Benefits of Internet of Things in Finance and Banking Security

Banks can enhance the security of their branch sites by implementing various security-focused technologies such as Closed-Circuit Television (CCTV) cameras, continuous security monitoring, intelligent alarm systems, and other similar measures. The relevance of the Internet of Things (IoT) lies in its ability to facilitate the interconnectivity and remote administration of various intelligent devices (Pandey, 2023). Consequently, in the event of a detected attack, the security team possesses the capability to promptly secure the branch or implement other requisite measures. When discussing the topic of mobile banking, it is important to acknowledge the significance of security concerns. The proliferation of sophisticated hacking techniques employed by cybercriminals has led to an escalation in cybersecurity threats, particularly in the banking sector. These risks pose a significant challenge as they target financial institutions' networks with the intent of illicitly acquiring valuable consumer information and monetary assets. According to Nasy (2023), the implementation of IoT in the banking industry offers the potential to safeguard personal data and mitigate the occurrence of errors or breaches. The authentication of user identities is a crucial component of contemporary financial services. Organisations employ diverse strategies to ensure the security of their systems and interconnected devices, encompassing biometric, visual, and auditory authentication techniques.

The paramount importance of security is evident in the financial sector. The foundation of the banking system primarily rests on the confidence individuals place in a bank's capacity to safeguard their financial resources. The implementation of Internet of Things (IoT) technology has the potential to enhance the foundational infrastructure of a bank's security system (xcube LABS, 2022). As an illustration, the Internet of Things (IoT) technology has the capability to collect data from a wide range of devices. The sole requirement is that the gadget possess the capability to transmit and receive network communications. Surveillance technologies such as Closed-Circuit Television (CCTV), smart alarms, and other monitoring equipment serve as valuable tools for data collection. The integration of these monitoring devices into an Internet of Things (IoT) network facilitates real-time monitoring (Chang *et al.* , 2020b). The transactional machines can also be equipped with Internet of Things (IoT) integration. The implementation of an IoT network can facilitate the process of system lockdown in the event of a security compromise.

Data Analytics

The field of data analytics involves the examination and interpretation of large sets of data in order to extract meaningful insights and make informed decisions. The Internet of Things (IoT) plays a crucial role in enhancing analytical capabilities across several industries. The Internet of Things (IoT) revolves around the collection and utilisation of data. The Internet of Things (IoT) network has the capability to collect an exceedingly large amount of data. The data is subsequently processed by specialised automated software, which generates valuable insights and information for the relevant industry. Financial institutions have the ability to utilise it as a means of collecting data pertaining to their customers. This information proves to be highly beneficial in the context of loan management (*et al.*, 2019). By leveraging IoT devices, such as sensors and smart metres, banks can gather real-time data on various economic indicators, such as property values, market trends, and consumer spending patterns. This data can then be analysed to assess the creditworthiness and financial stability of loan applicants, enabling banks to make more informed lending decisions. Additionally, an IoT network can facilitate the monitoring of loan collateral, such as real estate properties, by providing continuous updates on their condition and value. This enhanced monitoring capability can help banks mitigate risks associated with loan defaults and foreclosure. Overall, the integration of IoT technology in the banking sector offers significant potential for improving loan evaluation processes and enhancing risk management strategies. (LABS, 2022). The integration of Internet of Things (IoT) technology inside the banking sector enables the access and analysis of trading data from many sources. The trading volume of both private and government-issued bonds plays a crucial role in aiding banks in making more informed decisions pertaining to management. The utilisation of Internet of Things (IoT) technology in the banking sector facilitates the acquisition of up-to-date information regarding the initiatives or individuals that banks are providing financial support to. This enhanced access to data empowers banks to more accurately assess the Return On Investment (ROI) associated with their funding endeavours (Pandey, 2023). The implementation of the Internet of Things (IoT) in the banking sector, similar to its adoption in other industries, enhances analytical capabilities. The rapid growth of the financial technology (fintech) industry has resulted in an increasing volume of data being collected, analysed, and stored. An Internet of Things (IoT) network effectively manages the collection and processing of a substantial amount of data. According to Nasy (2023), the platform offers sophisticated analytics capabilities that provide a deeper comprehension of clients' behavioural patterns. The gathering of Internet of Things (IoT) data encompasses the retrieval of information from users' smart devices as well as other sources, such as social media platforms. The bank acquires valuable information through the process of system analysis.

Smart Wallets

Over the course of the previous decade, a multitude of wearable devices were developed with the capability to facilitate financial transactions. Fitness trackers, smart watches, wristbands, and jewellery possess intelligent functionalities. One potential benefit is the ability to remotely access credit card and checking accounts. These devices are capable of functioning independently. However, these platforms do not provide any customised functionality. The utilisation of the Internet of Things (IoT) is highly pervasive in these particular devices. Data is collected and modifications are made to specific characteristics based on individual habits. The utilisation of Internet of Things (IoT) technology in the banking sector has facilitated the expeditious completion of transactions through the implementation of these devices.

Continuously Monitoring

The practice of continuously monitoring a system or process in real-time. Internet of Things (IoT) devices have the capability to collect real-time data from the financial environment. According to Chang *et al.* (2020b), banks have the capability to assess the requirements of their customers at any given time or place by leveraging this data. One illustrative instance pertains to the estimation of the duration a consumer is expected to wait in a queue at a financial institution, such as a bank. Alternatively, a more advanced illustration could involve banks proactively contacting their consumers when their account balances are nearing depletion. Real-time data collection enables banks to offer data-accurate services

(Pandey, 2023). Process Automation Automated solutions have the potential to significantly enhance productivity within the banking sector. Financial institutions have the potential to utilise the Internet of Things (IoT) technology in order to establish automated processes that can effectively manage routine tasks (xcube LABS, 2022). Internet of Things (IoT) solutions have the potential to enhance the efficiency of smart devices. The Internet of Things (IoT) architecture serves as the fundamental framework for automated checkout systems. The implementation of Internet of Things (IoT) technology in the financial services industry has been instrumental in enhancing productivity through the automation of specific operational processes. The integration of technology in banking institutions enables the expedited processing of customer requests, the efficient opening of bank accounts, and the swift disabling of credit cards, all with minimal human participation. Consequently, this streamlined approach also minimises the occurrence of errors. The application of Internet of Things (IoT) technology within the banking sector extends beyond the mere facilitation of routine operational processes. Furthermore, clients have the capability to utilise Internet of Things (IoT) devices, like smartphones, to remotely access and unlock ATM doors beyond regular business hours. Internet of Things (IoT) systems possess the ability to respond to user requests, autonomously deactivate credit cards in cases of delayed payments, facilitate the transfer of asset ownership, and perform several other functions. The automation facilitated by the Internet of Things will enable the expeditious processing of loans and the effective monitoring of collateral.

Increased Effectiveness of Branch Banking

Upon the user's entry into the bank premises, biometric sensors will promptly commence the collection of his personal data, afterward transmitting this information to the central system for further processing and analysis. The implementation of smart branches offers bank managers the opportunity to save on maintenance and staffing costs, decrease client waiting times, and develop an interconnected communication network among branches located in diverse regions.

Enhanced Customer Experience

Currently, financial institutions place significant emphasis on enhancing the digital client experience. In contrast to earlier generations who exhibit satisfaction with conventional banking services, millennials and Zoomers demonstrate a greater propensity to switch banks in the event that their expectations are not met (Nasy, 2023). Hence, financial institutions make their utmost efforts to proactively anticipate the requirements of their customers. The adoption of the

Internet of Things (IoT) has a direct impact on customer engagement and the quality of service provided. Internet of Things (IoT) technologies facilitate the creation of comprehensive customer profiles within the banking sector. These profiles are constructed by gathering various data points, such as demographic information, significant life events, inter-client interactions, preferred services, historical records of declined bank offers, and frequently visited payment sites. By using these insightful findings, banking institutions can enhance their understanding of their clientele, discern their requirements, deliver tailored services and goods, and furnish pertinent financial aid and budgetary schemes (Chang *et al.* , 2020 b). The collection of data through connectivity devices enables banks to get valuable insights into the wants of their clients, hence facilitating the provision of enhanced services. The enhancement of clients' banking experiences can be achieved through the provision of timely information and the offering of personalised products. In addition, individuals visiting banks will have the capability to schedule appointments or check in using their cell phones, owing to the use of modern technology such as this. Additionally, this allows bank management to reduce both the workforce size and maintenance costs, resulting in decreased client waiting periods. Restructure Finance and Accounting Operations The successful collection of information in finance and accounting operations necessitates the participation of several departments. Instead of engaging in manual collaboration, firms have the option to fully automate the process. IoT devices enable the real-time collection and updating of information to the cloud. This practice facilitates the conservation of time and exertion that would otherwise be allocated to the compilation and administration of data from several teams.

Enhanced the Quality of Customer Service

The utilisation of Internet of Things (IoT) technology in the financial services sector contributes to the augmentation of customer service. Financial aid has the potential to enhance customer service through the implementation of intelligent and context-sensitive gadgets, which can facilitate the delivery of personalised messages and assist consumers upon their arrival. The utilisation of IoT technology is predominantly observed in the context of customer service. Internet of Things (IoT) collects user data and tracks a range of digital behaviours exhibited by individuals. The provided information holds significant value in the context of customer service. According to [x]cube LABS (2022), financial institutions have the ability to utilise this data in order to offer tailored customer care experiences to their clientele. The document will serve as a comprehensive record of the client's financial needs and preferences. Financial institutions have the capacity to utilise this information in order to propose budgetary strategies and other pertinent recommendations.

Enhanced Automated Teller Machines (ATMs)

Occasionally, contemporary automated teller machines (ATMs) may exhibit an appearance that is reminiscent of a previous era. Nevertheless, with the integration of ATMs with bank branches and the implementation of smartphone-controlled functionalities, the Internet of Things has the potential to revolutionise this particular encounter. By utilising motion sensors, individuals will have the capability to identify the nearest automated teller machine (ATM) in relation to their current location. A connected model will promptly communicate any malfunctions with the machine. This will facilitate efficient communication between a service provider and an engineer, hence reducing equipment downtime.

The Identification and Detection of Fraudulent Activities

There has been a global rise in the occurrence of banking fraud cases. The implementation of Internet of Things (IoT) technology has the potential to mitigate the occurrence of this catastrophic event. The implementation of Internet of Things (IoT) devices has already demonstrated a positive impact on enhancing the security of transactions. An illustration of this phenomenon is the current practice of mobile phones necessitating the utilisation of a user's biometric data in order to successfully carry out a transaction. According to Pandey (2023), there are websites that require consumers to input an authentication number sent by their banks to their mobile phones in order to verify their identity and authorise a purchase. The implementation of Internet of Things (IoT) technology has already enhanced the security of transactions and online purchases through the utilisation of biometric authentication and verification codes. According to Nasy (2023), mobile applications also collect information pertaining to the habits, preferences, and spending histories of their users. These observations can be utilised to identify atypical or questionable behaviour. As an illustration, in the event that an application detects a transaction as being fraudulent, the user would receive a timely notification, and their banking account would be temporarily deactivated. Instances of fraudulent actions are prevalent within the financial sector. The frequency of such accidents has experienced a significant increase over the course of the last decade. The implementation of Internet of Things (IoT) technology in the banking sector serves as a viable strategy to mitigate fraudulent activities. The implementation of a biometric system has the potential to significantly mitigate the prevalence of fraudulent actions. However, certain instances have a tendency to elude detection within the existing framework. The management of the Internet of Things (IoT) aids in the dissemination of information to clients on potential issues through the regular transmission of notifications following each transaction (x Cube LABS, 2022). Users have the ability to designate a transaction as fraudulent, resulting in the temporary suspension of their account while additional measures are taken. The expeditious response observed in the automated IoT system is attributable to the presence of real-time communication capabilities.

The utilisation of online banking applications that offer real-time notifications for every transaction serves as a conclusive example of how the Internet of Things (IoT) contributes to the identification and mitigation of fraudulent activities. This feature offers users the capability to closely monitor individual transactions, enabling them to promptly flag any unrecognised purchases as potential instances of fraud. The integration of Internet of Things (IoT) technology with artificial intelligence (AI)-driven analytics facilitates the detection of fraudulent activities and cyberattacks through the collection and examination of user account data (Shiklo, 2022). In the event that any suspicious behaviours are identified, the user will receive prompt notification, and their account will be temporarily suspended. The proliferation of digital banking services has resulted in an escalating incidence of fraudulent activities inside the financial industry. The emergence of novel data theft techniques can be attributed to the activities of hackers. The utilisation of the Internet of Things (IoT) in conjunction with analytics driven by artificial intelligence (AI) has proven to be a formidable asset in combating instances of bank fraud (Nasy, 2023).

Enhanced Quality of the Financial Service Encounter

Banking client services are influenced by the Internet of Things (IoT), as it provides customers with real-time data and a personalised experience. Due to the prevalence of connectivity, individuals visiting a certain establishment have the capability to arrange a scheduled meeting and subsequently confirm it using their smartphone device. By using this system, clients will be able to avoid waiting in queues since they will be promptly notified when it is their turn at the counter. In contrast, a service provider has the capability to monitor and record a client's past visits, the services they are presently availing of, and their most frequently raised queries. A prominent bank in India has successfully deployed an Internet of Things (IoT) beacon-based Bluetooth system, facilitating 24/7 access to automated teller machines (ATMs) for users.

One-Touch Payments

The concept of "one-touch payments" refers to a streamlined and simplified method of conducting financial transactions, wherein users are able to complete a payment. According to Shiklo (2022), the incorporation of banking Internet of Things (IoT) technologies and wearable devices enables customers to conduct payment transactions without the need to directly utilise their credit or debit cards.

NFC-enabled devices, such as smartphones and smartwatches, facilitate contactless payments, allowing for smooth and uninterrupted financial transactions.

Improved Customer Assistance

According to Shiklo (2022), banks possess the capability to customise their services for individual consumers by using data obtained *via* mobile applications, websites, and other platforms where transactions are executed and documented. The range of services provided would encompass personalised budgeting solutions and expert guidance on financial management.

Enhances Operational Effectiveness

The Internet of Things (IoT) facilitates the real-time monitoring of employee and corporate performance. Internet of Things (IoT) devices, like wearables, monitor and record the productive hours of teams, providing notifications in the event of any anomalies. Additionally, they offer data that can be used to assess the operational efficiency of equipment such as automated teller machines (ATMs) and consumer kiosks.

Additional Services

Money and asset management represent two prominent illustrations of contemporary banking practices. In recent times, financial institutions have begun leveraging data derived from customers' smart devices, including smartwatches, to assess and track their physical well-being (Pandey, 2023). The individuals will then be acknowledged for their daily routines and fitness regimens through the provision of cash-back incentives.

Customer Centrism

The concept of "customer centrism" refers to a business approach that places the customer at the centre of all decision-making processes and activities. In the midst of a significant digital upheaval, financial institutions are strategically leveraging the potential of the Internet of Things (IoT) to develop tailored products that align precisely with customer preferences. Several major banks globally are undergoing reorganisation of their front-office operations in response to an increased emphasis on customer centricity. Currently, the primary area of investment for banks' information technology (IT) is centered on enhancing the digital client experience, accounting for approximately 79% of their expenditure. Banks are actively responding to the mobile preferences expressed by technologically adept individuals belonging to Generation Z while concurrently upholding conventional services tailored to older clientele, such as phone banking.

Physical Cards

The concept of conducting transactions without the need for physical cards has gained significant attention in recent years. According to Shiklo (2022), contemporary mobile banking software has been designed to seamlessly integrate with credit and debit cards, hence streamlining the process of conducting transactions for users. This technology allows consumers to conduct contactless transactions by utilising their mobile devices. This particular function has facilitated the maintenance of hygiene in stores and other high-traffic locations, especially in the context of the pandemic.

Enhanced Expediency in Decision-Making

Numerous business decisions, such as investment decisions, rely on comprehensive data analytics, the study of business patterns, and market research. Organisations have the ability to leverage Internet of Things (IoT) devices in order to gather and analyse customer data, thereby acquiring significant insights into their preferences and requirements. This enables businesses to expedite the decision-making process. The integration of modern technologies, such as Artificial Intelligence (AI), with the Internet of Things (IoT) yields enhanced capabilities and potential in various domains, including banking. In order to facilitate strategic decision-making. By utilising Artificial Intelligence (AI), Machine Learning (ML), and Robotic Process Automation (RPA), financial executives can enhance their ability to analyse large datasets and make well-informed, strategic choices on resource allocation.

Challenges of IoTs in the Banking Sector

There remain various challenges associated with the implementation of Internet of Things (IoT) technologies across different domains. One of the primary obstacles faced by the Internet of Things (IoT) within the banking sector pertains to the safeguarding of both financial institutions and their clientele. The following examples represent a limited selection:

The Phenomenon of Data Compromises

In order to enhance the efficiency of their Internet of Things (IoT) devices and ecosystems, a significant number of banks have formed partnerships with prominent technology businesses. The occurrence of a data breach within any of these organisations has the potential to jeopardise the data privacy of banks and their clientele.

Privacy and Security Issues

Though IoT has some degree of security it sometimes has security challenges. Internet of Things (IoT) technologies provide enhanced security measures at the client level. However, the situation differs when it comes to financial institutions. The Internet of Things (IoT) is a rather nascent notion lacking established standards at present. However, a fundamental feature is the utilisation of several devices for the purpose of data collection ([x] Cube LABS, 2022). Proficient cybercriminals have the ability to manipulate the vulnerable security measures of interconnected devices, hence causing detrimental effects on the Internet of Things (IoT) network. While it is unlikely that individuals will engage in the act of stealing sensitive information, they possess the capability to manipulate the system in order to generate inaccurate feedback. The scope of this list of gadgets is extensive. Humans can possess a wide range of gadgets, such as intelligent safety sensors and ATM booths, among other examples. One limitation of this approach is the inherent difficulty in achieving uniform levels of security across all devices (xCube LABS, 2022). The potential for individuals to manipulate feedback gadgets and provide inaccurate data to the World Wide Web's Internet of Things (IoT) network is a notable concern. Within the realm of Financial Technology (Fintech), there exists a notable dearth of advancements in the preservation of crucial data confidentiality. Banks face a significant problem in effectively providing personalised consumer services with the Internet of Things (IoT). This is the reason why artificial intelligence (AI) is being employed in order to mitigate fraudulent activities within financial technology (Fintech) applications. The implementation of this measure contributes to the enhancement and optimisation of efforts to address the issue of cybercrime. The integration of Internet of Things (IoT) technology and financial technology (Fintech) devices, along with embedded artificial intelligence (AI), enables the collection of extensive client financial transaction data. This data acquisition facilitates enhanced security measures and streamlines financial processes, resulting in improved efficiency.

Deficiency in Standards

Every item possesses its unique maintenance methodology. The absence of standardised protocols for hardware maintenance in IoT devices can be attributed to the diverse range of manufacturers involved in their production. Regrettably, the potential cause of the malfunctioning of IoT devices could be attributed to the absence of universally accepted standards. The resolution of the issue at hand could potentially be achieved through the utilisation of equipment built by a single company. Nonetheless, the feasibility of this approach may be subject to practical limitations.

Redundancy

The concept of redundancy refers to the presence of unnecessary repetition or duplication within a particular system. The Internet of Things (IoT) generates a substantial volume of data, characterised by a significant magnitude. Undoubtedly, a sector of considerable size and dynamism, such as the banking industry, is expected to possess this characteristic. One notable aspect of data collected using such methodologies is that a significant proportion, approximately 90%, is deemed to lack utility or relevance. The majority of the data does not provide any advantageous information for financial institutions. According to [x]cube LABS (2022), a substantial amount of data processing will be required in order to extract the valuable components.

The Issue of Homogeneity

The Internet of Things (IoT) technology is considered to be in its nascent stage. Currently, there is a lack of universally accepted worldwide standards pertaining to the interface and compatibility of homogenous systems. Integrating devices from many manufacturers into a unified IoT network presents a significant challenge (xcube LABS, 2022).

Susceptible to Security Breaches/Exploitation

In the event that mobile banking applications are not consistently maintained and updated, there exists a potential vulnerability for hackers to exploit, resulting in the unauthorised access and misappropriation of the financial assets of numerous users. Alternatively, it is important to note that while an individual's applications may possess a certain level of security, their mobile devices, such as smartphones, may not exhibit the same level of protection. This further establishes a vulnerability through which unauthorised individuals can get access to and extract data.

The Handling of Data

The acquisition of user data from various devices poses a challenge in data management for financial service providers. It is imperative to effectively address the management of data and security concerns across several levels, encompassing both mobile applications and endpoint devices. Once an organisation has made the decision to incorporate Internet of Things (IoT) technology within the banking sector, it is imperative to acknowledge the substantial volume of data generated by IoT devices. Consequently, it becomes necessary to effectively store and analyse this data in order to enhance the overall client experience.

Applications of IoTs in the Banking and Finance Sectors

The utilisation of Internet of Things (IoT) technology in the banking and finance sector has emerged as a significant area of interest, with the aim of enhancing operational efficiency and customer experience.

Smart Branches

IoT solutions implemented in smart branches enhance the customer experience through several means, such as monitoring and managing queues, providing customers with real-time updates on estimated wait times, and directing them toward available service counters. According to Pandey (2023), the implementation of intelligent branches facilitates the sharing of user information, leading to operational streamlining and reduced staffing requirements.

Automated Teller Machine (ATM)

The retail banking sector has long employed a preliminary version of an Internet of Things (IoT) device known as the automated teller machine (ATM). Automated teller machines (ATMs) have emerged as prominent Internet of Things (IoT) devices, significantly enhancing the operational efficiency of banks. By facilitating instantaneous transactions, ATMs obviate the need for customers to rely on in-person interactions with bank tellers at physical branches (Insider Intelligence, 2022). The utilisation of Internet of Things (IoT) technology in the context of automated teller machines (ATMs) facilitates the establishment of a data flow system that empowers banks to effectively monitor consumer behaviour, discern patterns in ATM usage, and make informed decisions regarding the strategic placement of new ATMs in accordance with demand. The implementation of cost-saving operation modes necessitates the acquisition of data pertaining to the ATM site environment, such as room temperature, light intensity, and motion, through the utilisation of Internet of Things (IoT) sensors. Modifying the lighting conditions at an automated teller machine (ATM) location in accordance with the level of pedestrian activity can result in reduced energy usage (Pandey, 2023). Internet of Things (IoT) solutions play a crucial role in facilitating the management of various events, including the utilisation of skimming devices, card reader malfunctions, cash shortages, and similar occurrences. This is achieved through the provision of real-time monitoring capabilities for ATM operations and cash levels (Shiklo, 2022).

Trade financing

Trade finance refers to the financial instruments and products that facilitate international trade transactions. It encompasses a range of activities, such as providing financing. The implementation of Internet of Things (IoT) technology enables banks involved in trade financing to utilise real-time data for decision-making purposes, while simultaneously maintaining transparency on the physical movements that they are providing financial support. According to Pandey (2023), the utilisation of data generated by the Internet of Things (IoT) enables banks to enhance their fund management, expand their financing strategies, and improve their risk assessment capabilities across the trade life cycle.

Insurance

Insurance is a risk management strategy that involves the transfer of potential financial loss from one individual or group to another. Internet of Things (IoT) devices are designed to monitor the status of insured products and promptly inform insurers of any irregularities. This enables insurers to respond and implement appropriate measures to mitigate risks (Shiklo, 2022). Insurance businesses leverage data created by the Internet of Things (IoT) to forecast occurrences and formulate proactive measures. According to Pandey (2023), an insurance company has the potential to detect an asset malfunction and notify the policyholder in advance to prevent any resulting harm. This particular method facilitates the mitigation of insurance claims and serves as a safeguard against instances of insurance fraud.

Auditing and Accounting

The integration of Internet of Things (IoT) technology in the communication between the client's payment systems and the software used by Certified Public Accountants (CPAs) allows for the automation of various routine bookkeeping processes, including but not limited to data entry, reconciliation, and invoicing. The Internet of Things (IoT) facilitates the ability of accountants to actively monitor financial data in real-time, enabling them to gain accurate and detailed insights into the operational aspects of a firm. This enhanced access to information empowers accountants to effectively fulfill their advisory responsibilities (Shiklo, 2022; Charles *et al.* , 2023). The implementation of the Internet of Things (IoT) has been found to enhance transparency and automation in the field of auditing. This advancement enables Certified Public Accountants (CPAs) to effectively oversee transactions and promptly handle audit trails, thereby facilitating the identification of data anomalies and the prevention of fraudulent activities.

Used Cases of IoTs in Finance and banking Smart Contracts

The issue of security and privacy is a paramount worry for consumers, irrespective of their age demographic. According to a report by Insider Intelligence (2022), the Internet of Things (IoT) has facilitated the integration of blockchain technology inside the banking sector, hence enhancing customer authentication processes. Insider Intelligence (2022) asserts that the use of blockchain for identity authentication has the advantage of immutable identity credentials, as once recorded, they are impervious to modification or tampering.

Wearable Technology

A significant number of individuals use smartwatches and other wrist-worn electronic devices. According to Pandey (2023), banks have the potential to enhance accessibility and convenience for clients by creating an online application that is compatible with wearable devices. Clients have the ability to keep track of their heart rates, engage in professional email correspondence, and carry out cash transactions using the same device. The Internet of Things (IoT) has facilitated the proliferation of wearables and intelligent speech devices across various industries, including the banking sector. According to a report by Insider Intelligence (2022), there is a notable trend among consumers towards the adoption of smart devices, which in turn presents significant opportunities for growth within the banking industry. Wearable devices have the ability to strengthen security measures by providing clients with real-time notifications if there is a withdrawal of funds from their accounts. Customers also have the ability to engage in communication with banks through the utilisation of their wearable gadgets. This feature enables the execution of multiple tasks simultaneously and optimises time management for clients. The availability of easy and immediate access to one's budget through a smart device can also aid clients in attaining their financial goals and fostering savings.

Mobile Wallets

The concept of mobile wallets refers to digital platforms that enable individuals to store and manage their financial information, such as credit card details. Over the course of the preceding centuries, there have been substantial transformations in monetary systems. People choose to exchange real gold for currencies that are supported by banks. Over time, physical currency was substituted by electronic cards that granted individuals the ability to access digital funds through online platforms. The advent of mobile wallets has significantly advanced the realm of currency, enabling clients to conveniently manage their financial transactions by using the dedicated wallet application and utilising their smartphones for contactless payments (Pandey, 2023). Mobile wallets offer a high level of convenience, allowing clients to reduce the number of physical objects they need to carry on a daily basis. In contemporary society, a significant proportion of people possess a smartphone, thereby reflecting the prevalence of digital technology. The adaptation of banking technology for utilisation of mobile devices has emerged as a highly pragmatic advancement in the realm of the Internet of Things (IoT) within the banking industry. It is imperative for customers to prioritise the safeguarding of their mobile devices in order to ensure the security of phone-based payment transactions.

The Implementation of Heightened Security Measures In the foreseeable future, blockchain technology is anticipated to exert a significant impact on the banking sector. According to Pandey (2023), this emerging technology allows individuals to engage in secure transactions without the need for an intermediary, which is traditionally fulfilled by financial institutions. Nevertheless, financial institutions have the potential to leverage blockchain technology as a means to enhance the security of their clients. Blockchain technology is particularly advantageous in the context of international transactions. The permanent recording of every action poses challenges to the commission of fraudulent activities. The adoption of blockchain technology by banks has the potential to effectively decrease operational costs while simultaneously enhancing consumer transparency in a secure manner. Furthermore, the implementation of blockchain technology has the potential to enhance customer identification processes and provide enhanced security measures for safeguarding client assets.

Smart Piggybanks

The concept of smart piggybanks refers to technologically advanced devices that are designed to enhance the traditional function of piggybanks. Smart piggybanks represent a further advancement in the realm of Internet of Things (IoT) banking innovations. Currently, financial institutions provide virtual piggy bank services to aid customers in efficiently defining and attaining their financial objectives. This application provides an engaging platform for young children to actively participate in the realm of financial management. The digital iteration of a traditional piggy bank incorporates interest rates, facilitating the accelerated growth of one's funds. This vintage-inspired advancement is equally efficacious for individuals of mature age. The term "investment banking" may be perceived as daunting by certain individuals, while "online piggybank" conveys a sense of simplicity and user-friendliness. The Internet of Things (IoT) facilitates the ability of banks to engage in rebranding efforts and broaden their customer base, thereby leading to financial advantages for both the banks themselves and their clientele.

Future of Internet of Things in Finance and Banking

The banking sector perpetually seeks novel avenues for expansion. There exist a multitude of crucial trends that are poised to exert the most substantial influence on the sector in the forthcoming years. The Internet of Things (IoT) is considered to be one such technological advancement. This technology holds significant potential for the future and plays a crucial role in the ongoing digital evolution of the banking sector. The Internet of Things (IoT) presents a significant opportunity for banks, insurance companies, and fintech firms to foster innovation within their respective industries. Financial companies have effectively incorporated Internet of Things (IoT) systems into their daily operations. However, there are numerous untapped avenues for future advancement in this domain. However, the trajectory of the Internet of Things (IoT) in the banking sector will predominantly hinge upon the expeditious resolution of prevailing implementation challenges. These challenges are prevalent throughout various disciplines. Banks are encountering similar challenges within their systems as they endeavour to enhance security measures on the client side. The utilisation of several devices for data collection introduces heightened vulnerability to cyberattacks, hence compromising security. Furthermore, a portion of the data obtained from various sources lacks utility. Furthermore, it is important to note that the aforementioned practice might potentially have negative consequences for those seeking a loan. Additionally, it is worth considering that the health-related information of these individuals has the potential to influence the interest rate associated with their loans. However, it is worth noting that the Internet of Things (IoT) plays a significant role in the evolution of the finance business, enabling it to surpass the limitations of traditional banking practices. The implementation of this concept has been accomplished through many methods, offering novel approaches to enhance operational efficiency. In the forthcoming years, banks are expected to accelerate their transition towards digitalization in order to enhance their market presence.

Implications

This chapter examines the application of Internet of Things (IoT) technology within the financial and banking industries. This study examines the advantages and obstacles associated with the implementation of Internet of Things (IoT) technology in the banking industry. There are numerous consequences for bankers and managers in relation to the Internet of Things (IoT) in the finance sector. Although the IoT has gained significant recognition as a prevailing trend, it still possesses substantial potential for further advancement in the future. Several anticipated trends in the Internet of Things (IoT) are expected to significantly enhance the Fintech industry. These trends encompass the development of sophisticated IoT platforms, alterations in the design of operating systems, and advancements in device architecture. The growth of the fintech sector has resulted in a rise in privacy issues and obstacles for industry professionals and management. It is recommended that managers and bankers employ the Internet of Things (IoT) in order to establish connections across systems through the utilisation of artificial intelligence (AI), thereby safeguarding against potential data breaches, manipulation, and fraudulent activities. Another noteworthy potentiality is the production of data; the Internet of Things (IoT) will facilitate the management of data streams containing a substantial volume of entries by enabling the implementation of real-time analytics. The Internet of Things (IoT) possesses significant transformative potential in the banking and financial services industry, promising a promising outlook for the future. The significant technology revolution will enable individuals to optimise their time, enhance productivity, and adopt a more convenient way of living. While the implementation of the Internet of Things (IoT) in the banking sector is now in the initial planning phase, there is significant potential for innovative advancements within this domain. It has the potential to impact several facets, encompassing the augmentation of business revenue as well as the enhancement of customer service provisions.

The financial industry is assuming greater importance in contemporary times. In the future, it is anticipated that retail banking, core banking, and other financial software will undergo transformation as well. The integration of client management, business automation, and transformed transactions has demonstrated the efficacy of the Internet of Things (IoT) in the financial technology (Fintech) sector. In the realm of banking, the utilisation of Internet of Things (IoT) data facilitates a smoother shift from conventional procedures to contemporary ones, hence enhancing consumer experiences. Banking professionals possess the ability to perceive. Fintech and banking institutions are venturing beyond their customary boundaries in order to embrace Internet of Things (IoT) technology and establish themselves as frontrunners in the industry. There is a growing need for managers to utilise the Internet of Things (IoT) in order to convert data into practical insights that facilitate improved decision-making.

CONCLUSION

The objective of this chapter is to examine the domain of Internet of Things (IoT) development and its influence on the banking and financial services sectors. This study examines the advantages and obstacles associated with the implementation of Internet of Things (IoT) technology in the banking industry. The advent of Internet of Things (IoT) technology has presented numerous prospects for the future of banking and financial services. The Internet of Things (IoT) revolution possesses the potential to enhance the efficiency, sustainability, and cost-effectiveness of contemporary industries. To fully leverage the potential of IoT technology, decision-makers might benefit from doing a cost-benefit analysis to evaluate the feasibility of implementing IoT in various sectors. The companies that excel in the field of IoT are those that possess a deep understanding of how to seamlessly integrate IoT technology into their products, thereby differentiating themselves from their conventional competitors. While individuals who possess the necessary skills and abilities are generally able to navigate life's challenges, those who lack such capabilities are often compelled to engage in physical confrontations in order to ensure their survival. It is advantageous for firms to allocate resources towards investing in the Internet of Things (IoT) and prioritising its development, given the projected rapid advancement of IoT in the coming decade. Several technological challenges are associated with the Internet of Things (IoT). These challenges include identity management, energy-efficient sensing, greening IoT, scalability, security and privacy, communication mechanisms, integration of smart components, and worldwide cooperation. The scientific issues encompass the need for interoperability, efficient management of ambiguous information, and service adaptability within a dynamic system environment. The Internet of Things (IoT) has significantly enhanced convenience and connectivity in contemporary society. In order to enhance customer service, financial institutions are incorporating Internet of Things (IoT) technologies into their user interfaces and applications. Furthermore, this technology aids in safeguarding the assets of clients and facilitating the expansion of their business ventures beyond the realm of banking. Banks are employing Internet of Things (IoT) technology in diverse applications to enhance their service offerings. The utilisation of Internet of Things (IoT) technology enables bank customers to conveniently employ mobile wallets, enhances security measures through the implementation of blockchain technology, and expedites the process of saving money by means of smart piggybanks. The finance sector is currently experiencing a significant technological transformation. A plethora of novel technologies are always undergoing testing and integration across many industries. While several technological advancements garner significant notoriety, others fail to achieve the same level of acclaim. However, it appears that the implementation of Internet of Things (IoT) technology in the financial sector has the potential to significantly alter the existing landscape.

REFERENCES

Atzori, L., Iera, A., Morabito, G. (2010). The Internet of Things: A survey. *Comput. Netw., 54*(15), 2787-2805.
[http://dx.doi.org/10.1016/j.comnet.2010.05.010]

Avasalcai, C., Tsigkanos, C., Dustdar, S. (2019). Decentralized Resource Auctioning for Latency-Sensitive Edge Computing. *IEEE International Conference on Edge Computing (EDGE).*
[http://dx.doi.org/10.1109/EDGE.2019.00027]

Arslanian, H., Fischer, F. (2019). The Future of Finance: The Impact of Fintech, AI, and Crypto on Financial Services. *Chapter.*

[http://dx.doi.org/10.1007/978-3-030-14533-0]

Arslanian, H., Fischer, F. (2019). Fintech and the Future of the Financial Ecosystem. *Future Finance.* [http://dx.doi.org/10.1007/978-3-030-14533-0_16]

Arslanian, H., Fischer, F. (2019). Blockchain as an Enabling Technology. *Future Finance*, 113–121.

Arslanian, H., Fischer, F., 2019. The Emergence of Techfin. *Future Finance*, 69–75. [http://dx.doi.org/10.1007/978-3-030-14533-0_10]

Baranovskyi, O. I. (2020). Regulation of functional and structural transformational processes in the financial sector. *Financial and credit activity: problems of theory and practice, 1*(32), 292-306.

Chang, Y., Iakovou, E., Shi, W. (2020). Blockchain in global supply chains and cross border trade: a critical synthesis of the state-of-the-art, challenges and opportunities. *Int. J. Prod. Res., 58*(7), 2082-2099. b [http://dx.doi.org/10.1080/00207543.2019.1651946]

Charles, A., Yomboi, J., Arko-Cole, N., Tijani, A. (2023). Emerging Use of Technologies in Education. *Digital Transformation in Education: Emerging Markets and Opportunities, 82.*

Grivas, S.G., Schürch, R., Giovanoli, C. (2016). How Cloud Will Transform the Retail Banking Industry. *Proceedings of the 6th International Conference on Cloud Computing and Services Science.* [http://dx.doi.org/10.5220/0005910903020309]

Kumari, S., Kulkarni, S., Patil, N., Deshpande, V. (2020). An Internet of Things (IoT) Based Implementation of Smart Digital City Prototype. *Third International Conference on Smart Systems and Inventive Technology (ICSSIT).* [http://dx.doi.org/10.1109/ICSSIT48917.2020.9214157]

Maiti, M., Ghosh, U. (2021). Next Generation Internet of Things in Fintech Ecosystem. *IEEE Internet Things J., 1-8.

Marafie, Z., Lin, K.-J., Zhai, Y., Li, J., (2018). ProActive Fintech: Using Intelligent IoT to Deliver Positive InsurTech Feedback. In: *IEEE 20th Conference on Business Informatics*, pp. 72–81.

Miskiewicz, R. (2020). Internet of Things in Marketing: Bibliometric Analysis. *Marketing and Management of Innovations, 3*, 371-381. [http://dx.doi.org/10.21272/mmi.2020.3-27]

Mick, T., Tourani, R., Misra, S. (2018). LASeR: Lightweight Authentication and Secured Routing for NDN IoT in Smart Cities. *IEEE Internet Things J., 5*(2), 755-764. [http://dx.doi.org/10.1109/JIOT.2017.2725238]

Nasy, J. (2023). IoT in Banking: Examples of IoT technology used in financial services. Available from: https://limestonedigital.com/iot-in-banking-examples-of-iot-technology-used-in-financial-services/.

Olsen, T.L., Tomlin, B. (2020). Industry 4.0: Opportunities and Challenges for Operations Management. *Manuf. Serv. Oper. Manag., 22*(1), 113-122. [http://dx.doi.org/10.1287/msom.2019.0796]

Pandey, P. (2023). What is IoT in Banking? Meaning, Advantages, Applications, and more. Available from: https://sabpaisa.in/blog/iot-in-banking/#:~:text=IoT%20technology%20is%20being%20used,money%20faster%20with%20smart%20piggybanks.

Shiklo, B. (2022). IoT for Smart Banking and Finance. Available from: https://www.scnsoft.com/blog/iot-i--banking-and-financial-services.

Insider Intelligence, (2022). IoTs in Banking: Examples of IoT technology used in financial services. Available from: https://www.insiderintelligence.com/insights/iot-banking/.

Wamba, S.F., Queiroz, M.M. (2020). Industry 4.0 and the supply chain digitalisation: a blockchain diffusion perspective. *Prod. Plann. Contr., 1-18.

Cube LABS, (2022). The Applications Of IoT In The Banking Industry. Available from: https://www.xcubelabs.com/blog/the-applications-of-iot-in-the-banking-industry/.

Yomboi, J., Nangpiire, C., Kutochigaga, E.A., Majeed, M. (2021). The impact of the collapsed banks on customers in Ghana. *Asian Journal of Economics. Asian Journal of Economics, Business and Accounting, 21*(17), 15-25.
[http://dx.doi.org/10.9734/ajeba/2021/v21i1730487]

SUBJECT INDEX